Pentacle Book of Pagan Knowledge

MARION PEARCE

GREEN MAGIC

Pentacle Book of Pagan Knowledge © 2025 by Marion Pearce. All rights reserved. No part of this book may be used or reproduced in any form without written permission of the Author, except in the case of quotations in articles and reviews.

Green Magic
Seed Factory
Aller
Langport
Somerset
TA10 0QN
England

www.greenmagicpublishing.com

Cover image by kind permission of
Linda Ravenscroft
www.lindaravenscroft.com

Designed and typeset by Carrigboy, Wells, UK.
www.carrigboy.co.uk

ISBN 9781915580276

GREEN MAGIC

Contents

Aspects of Anglo-Saxon Paganism Pete Jennings	5
Black Shuck and the Wild Hunt Pete Jennings	13
Borderlands: Fairy and Liminality in the Scottish Lowlands Kevin Manwaring	17
Irish Druidry and the Modern Druid Movement Luke Eastwood	30
Isles of the Dead Kevin Mainwaring	36
Lewis Bonfire Night Celebrations Marion Pearce	44
Seriously Modern Dragons: More than a Myth Lucya Starza	49
The Occult War: Secret Agents, Magicians and Hitler Michael Howard	53
The Old Ones in the Old Book Philip West	76

The Web of Wyrd and the Runes   84
Nigel Pennick

The Magic of the Thracians is still Alive ...   91
Georgi Mishev

Witchcraft and the Monarchy   97
Richard Simpson

Witchcraft before Wicca   109
Michael Howard

The Sprit of the Woods: The Welsh Tradition of Myrddin/Merlin   117
August Hunt

Aspects of Anglo-Saxon Paganism

PETE JENNINGS

Whilst Anglo-Saxons living alongside Heathen Norsemen in the Danelaw area may have been influenced to return to their religious roots, I deplore the way in which it is presumed by many that Anglo-Saxon Paganism was the same as Scandinavian but with some slight name changes (Odin to Woden, Thor to Thunor, Tyr to Tiw, etc.). In fact, as someone with an interest in Norse Paganism as well, it was not very consistent from one village to the next, let alone across several different countries. Let's not fall into the archaeologist trap: "If we can't explain it, it must have a ritual purpose!" So much is unknown, uncertain, and down to individual interpretation.

A lot of emphasis has been placed upon the writings of the Venerable Bede, England's first historian, in Jarrow after the Christianisation of England. Whilst he does provide some excellent evidence regarding some Anglo-Saxon Heathen practices, such as the origins of calendar terms, including mentioning the obscure Heathen deities Eostre, Hretha (month names) & Saetere (giving us Saturday), one must remember that he was a Christian monk with a political viewpoint, especially regarding the lineage and legitimacy of his current royal dynasty and culture. That makes it all the more surprising that he should remind us that the Heathen feast of Modranicht is arguably on the 26th December, and that the months Solmonath (Feb) is a feast of cakes, September is named as Halegmonath (holymonth), and November is Blotmonath for animal sacrifices. Why would a Christian cleric want to make these up?

We have a far wider range of powerful literature, in the form of texts that can be analysed for clues to our Heathen past: heroic poetry such as *Beowulf and the Battle of Maldon*, material from leechbooks and verse charms (such as the *Nine Herbs Charm*), laws, the *Anglo-Saxon Chronicle*, letters, and the Anglo-Saxon rune poem. I would argue that you cannot get into the early Anglo-Saxon mindset without understanding something of the Paganism of that period, even when it had officially ceased to exist.

According to the sixth century writer Gildas, the first of the Heathen Saxon fifth century newcomers were allegedly Hengist and Horsa, two Saxon brother warrior leaders brought in by the Celt Vortigen to evict the Picts between about 449–456CE. After completing this mercenary task, they decided to stay on, against his wishes. At a battle near Ashingdon in Kent, Horsa was killed, and the still visible White Horse Stone (or possibly its replacement) is said to be where he is buried, and is thus an important place to modern Heathens as a memorial to one of the two human sources of English Heathenism. It lies off the A229 Maidstone-Chatham road, near to where the Pilgrims Way and the more modern Channel Tunnel link cross it. It can be found via a footpath near to a garage.

Consider briefly the names though: Vortigen is less a name than a title, which has been interpreted as 'King of Kings', Horsa means 'horse', and Hengist 'stallion' or alternatively the almost opposite 'gelding' (how etymologists justify their art as a science sometimes eludes me!). How likely is it for two sons both to be named after equine fashion? I wonder whether these were titles, rather than names, in the same way that Emperor Haile Selasie of Ethiopia was known as the 'Lion of Judah'?

LAWS

Whilst I will accept that some laws are copied from one king to another, the successive laws against Paganism seem to subtly change focus in each new generation, presumably to combat whatever is the latest fad. The Saxon royalty and church give us evidence of what was going on in England by what they forbade. For example, The Laws of King Alfred include:

> "30. The women (femnan) who are accustomed to harbor enchanters (onfon gealdor-creftigan) and wizards (scinlecan) and witches (wiccan) do not allow them to live …
> 32. And he that sacrifices to idols (god-geldum on saeage), rather than to God alone, let him suffer death" (Griffiths, 2006, p50).

Hence, we know that people in the 880s were acting as enchanters, wizards, and witches, as well as sacrificing to idols – it is unlikely that a law be passed against something that didn't exist. Prior to that, in 666CE, the biographer of St. Wilfred says how a priest of the South Saxons cursed Wilfred and his companions as they were cast ashore in a storm:

> "The Council of Clofeshoh (747) condemned those who practiced divinations, auguries, incantations, and the like. The Dialogue of Archbishop Egbert named those who worshipped idols or gave themselves to the Devil through others who took auspices or practiced astrology or enchantment as men who should never be appointed to the priesthood" (Blair, P.H., 1997, p117).

One might think they were already part of a rival priesthood, and wouldn't be interested in the one being denied them!

Between 1009–16CE, King Ethelred published his laws, which included "renounce all Pagan customs" (Griffiths, 2006, p84), demonstrating that this was still a problem within an Anglo-Saxon culture that had supposedly been converted to Christianity nearly four centuries previously, when there was specific banning of Pagan practices by Archbishop Theodore's seventh century *Paenitentiale*, including penances for sacrificing to devils and foretelling the future and burning grain in a house after the death of a man. That is the only reference I know of that particular Pagan practice.

The popular image of Christian conversion across Europe is not supported by the evidence, with some countries alternating between various religions, dependant on their rulers, invaders and even who they wanted as their allies or trading partners. Why, for instance, was the supposedly Christian King Æthelhere of the East Angles named by Bede as being within the ill-fated 30 legions of the fervently Heathen King Penda's expedition in 654AD to attack Oswin (Stenton, 1971, p83)? Was it purely politics or had East Anglia reverted back to Paganism again? Prudence Jones & Nigel Pennick provide a detailed analysis of this type of process in *A History of Pagan Europe* (1995). Earlier, East Anglian King Raedwald had been baptised in Kent, but added a crucifix to his Heathen temple and had a massive treasure burial – hardly the expected action of a Christian. Maybe, like Prince Charles, he wanted to be 'Defender of the Faiths' to his multi-faith society. The Prittlewell treasure grave has proved this type of ostentatious funeral wasn't unique in this period.

Wulfstan, Aelric, and King Cnut (995CE) collectively banned animal guising, saluting the moon, making offerings at waterfalls and trees, making oaths to Heathen gods, etc. in edicts years apart, which suggests it was still continuing. King Edgar had already forbidden well worship, divination, and practices around trees and wells in about 970CE, only 25 years before Cnut. It would seem unlikely that laws would be repeatedly passed against some action that no longer happened. Of course, these accounts do all give us a very clear idea of what we should do as modern Heathens if we wish to worship in the way that our ancestors did.

RITUALS & MAGIC

If one examines Anglo-Saxon charms, such as the one to make a field fruitful (Erce), it is hard to deny that there are some very magical acts going on alongside the instruction to say the Lord's Prayer (cutting turf and putting herbs and grain into the soil, etc.). The period may officially be Christian, but it seems a lot of the old ways lingered, in a form semi acceptable to the new religion.

When King Aethelbert, in around 597CE, at Thanet in Kent, meets some 40 Christian missionaries, including Augustine, he insists that it be in the open because he is suspicious of their magic. Does that mean then that at that place and time people believed magic could only take place indoors?

CULT CENTRES

Whilst there will always be linguistic and etymological arguments around place names, some of them give evidence of centres of religious cults. Wansdyke, Wednesbury (Wodens Barrow), Wednesfield, Thundersley (Thunors Grove), and Thurstable (Thunors Pillar) which suggests a link with the sacred Irminsul pillars on the continent destroyed by Charlemagne; but St. Anselm commenting on Heathen temples in Wessex mentions also that those "crude pillars (ermula) of the same foul snake and the stag were worshipped with coarse stupidity in profane shrines" (Thompson, 2004, p19). It was a stag that surmounted the whetstone sceptre of Sutton Hoo, despite the wolf element to the Wuffingas Dynasty clan name.

Other examples include Tysoe (Tiws Hill Spur), and place names with an original element of hearh (= hill sanctuary) in them, such as Harrow Hill, indicating an outdoor altar site. Weoh (= ido, allegedly) forms a Pagan element of place names, such as Wayland Wood. What is much more controversial is the use of the Grimr nickname for Woden as part of place names. Whilst Grimsby might have been a centre for his worship, some places such as Grim's Dyke, Grimspound, Grime's Graves, etc. may have been named by later generations after a being that had by then gained 'bogeyman' status. What hasn't had much attention given to it in recent years is the idea of areas named after their original tribes, who in turn had people ruling them who could only do so by claiming direct lineage back to a Pagan deity, such as Woden or Seaxnot – and study of Frank Stenton (1971) will still repay the effort.

TEMPLES

According to Bede, the Anglo-Saxon Heathen priest Coifi was asked by King Edwin of Northumbria to persuade the people to convert to Christianity in 627CE, by setting an example. He carried a spear on a stallion and threw it into the temple (ealh = temple) at Goodmanham in the East Riding of Yorkshire, all taboo acts for an Anglo-Saxon Heathen priest (Blair, P., 1977, p121). In contrast, at least one Icelandic priest owned a stallion, and none seemed barred from carrying arms. They did share the custom of not taking weapons into the temple.

Certainly, there must have been some well-constructed Heathen temples in England. Why else would Pope Gregory write to Abbot Mellitus a letter dated 17th June, 601 (quoted by Bede), instructing him:

> "I have come to the conclusion that the temples of the idols in England should not on any account be destroyed. Augustine must smash the idols, but the temples themselves should be

sprinkled with holy water and altars set up in them in which relics are to be enclosed. For we ought to take advantage of well-built temples by purifying them from Devil worship" (Branston, B., 1974, p54).

Those English Heathen temples must have flourished well into the era of Christian conversion, since elsewhere Bede mentions:

"An unbroken tradition of at least one Heathen temple seen by King Aldwulf of East Anglia 'who lived into our own times' and who testified that 'this temple was still standing in his day, and that he had seen it when a boy.' It had belonged to Aldwulf's predecessor, King Redwald" (Branston, B., 1974, p54).

The King Raedwald in question died in about 625CE, and is believed to be the main burial at Sutton Hoo. His temple was probably where Rendlesham Church now stands in Suffolk. If the life of Eadwulf (Aldwulf) is taken as 664–713CE, and if he saw it when he was six years old (the earliest he is likely to recollect), then it was there in 670–45 years after the death of Raedwald and, supposedly, Heathen practice. Bede writes about King Sighere of the East Saxons rebuilding ruined temples to restore Heathen worship after a serious plague in 665CE.

DANCE

A plate on the side of the Sutton Hoo helmet shows what appear to be two figures, each dancing with two spears and a sword, across two crossed spears on the ground. They have elaborate helmets on that appear to be crested with large bird-ended horns. There is a similar figure shown on the Finglesham Belt Buckle from Kent, and they have close parallels with cast bronze plates from Torslunda, Sweden. It appears that ritual dancing is going on and the Ormsgard Dark Ages Re-Enactment theatre group had been trying to do some experimental archaeology around that at Sutton Hoo in 2008. Whilst one can argue about what sort of ritual dance it is, it would be hard to put it into a Christian context.

Two of the figures from the Torslunda plates have helmets with boars on them, and at least two similar helmets have been found in England: Bently Grange, Derbyshire, and fragments at Woolaston, Northants and Guilden Morden, Cambs. Whilst they could simply be decoration, are they evidence of a boar cult, which is the animal sacred to Frey? As I indicated at the start of this piece, and return to at its end – it is all down to interpretation.

This article was based on a talk and article previously published in *Widowinde*, the journal of Da Engliscan Gesioas (The English Companions). For more information on this Anglo-Saxon society, send a S.A.E. to: English Companions, BM Box 4336, London, WC1X 3XX.

The article draws upon some material from Pete Jennings' book, *Heathen Paths: Viking and Anglo-Saxon Pagan Beliefs* (Capall-Bann Press, 2007). Pete Jennings homepages are at: www.gippeswic.demon.co.uk

OTHER REFERENCES:

Blair, P. (1997) *An Introduction to Anglo-Saxon England* 2nd Edition. Cambridge: Cambridge University Press.
Branston, B. (1974) *The Lost Gods of England*. London: Book Club Associates.
Griffiths, B. (2006) *Early English Law: An Introduction*. Swaffham: Anglo-Saxon Books.
Jones, P. and Pennick, N. (1995) *A History of Pagan Europe*. London: Routledge.
Ormsgard Dark Ages Re-Enactment website: www.ormsgard.org

Black Shuck and the Wild Hunt

PETE JENNINGS

I have long been fascinated by the stories of Black Shuck in East Anglia. He is said to be a devil dog, black, shaggy-haired and enormous with fiery red eyes the size of saucers. There are two popular stories of him entering churches at St. Marys, Bungay and All Saints, Blythburgh. You can see a burnt claw mark on the north door of the latter church accredited to him. The Bungay incident of the 4th August, 1577, was written up by Abraham Fleming in a blackletter pamphlet. Although it was August, there was said to be a thunderstorm overhead at the time. A man and a boy in the congregation were killed; as a psychopomp, there is a belief that looking directly into Black Shuck's saucer-like fiery eyes will cause death or disaster either instantly, or within a twelvemonth. At Blythburgh, part of the tower crashed down, and again two of the congregation were killed.

Sightings seem to never be more than a few miles inland from the East Coast, and range from mainly marshy, wet places in Maldon and around East Anglia, up as far as York (Viking Jorvik), where he is known as the barghuest. Other names include Galleytrot, Padfoot, Old Shug, and others. There has been a theory that maybe he is the remnant of a fylga (fetch) sent to clear the coastal paths for raiding Vikings. Of course, it is speculation, but personally I find it at least possible – the locations all fall within the old Danelaw area.

The name Shuck is believed to be of Anglo-Saxon origin – 1,000 years before the Bungay and Blythburgh incidents. It is thought to derive from the word *scucca*, meaning demon. The term is also used to describe Grendel and his mother in the Anglo-Saxon poem *Beowulf*. They are two monsters who dwell in marshland, have glowing eyes; and Dr. Sam Newton has pointed out that the East Anglian dialect word *grindle*, which is preserved in some Suffolk place names, means a drainage ditch or wet place – so this could be the origin of the name Grendel, as a creature who lives on the marsh.

Back in the 1970s, an elderly chap used to visit the Butley Oyster pub in Suffolk, where I used to go for singing sessions on Sunday nights. He arrived as white as a sheet one weekday night, and said that he had been pushing his bike downhill, on the way to the pub, when he had encountered a large spectral dog. Being generally afraid of dogs, he had just kept going (and not stared in its eyes), but the beast went straight through him. Another old chap bought him a brandy to settle his nerves. This was commented upon afterwards as proof of how ill he looked – his benefactor had never been known to ever buy a drink for anyone else before!

Some say he is a hound of Wotan's Wild Hunt (or Anglo-Saxon *herlathing*) who can be heard howling on the wintry winds and seeking lost souls at the darker time of year. Monks at Peterborough commented upon it in 1132, and believed it was a response to the appointment of a bad abbot. Another twelfth-century writer, Walter Map, also describes the *herlathing*, which he related to a real person, mistaking a nickname for Odin/Wotan for a leader called Herle (*thing* denotes a group of people in Old English). St. Guthlac, who lived as a hermit on an island in the fens at Crowland in the early eighth century, not far from Peterborough, was also beset by spectral creatures attacking him, after upsetting them by singing Christian psalms. This is the same sort of reason that was blamed for Grendel attacking the hall in Beowulf, and yet more evidence linking the poem with an East Anglian origin (see the Dr. Sam Newton book for a full investigation of that).

Of course, there are other legends of supernatural hunters around Britain, from Herne at Windsor to the Gabriel Hounds of the West Country, and further afield across Europe (I love the Danish legend of a hunt pursuing Slattenpat, an ugly old woman whose name translates as 'wobbly boob'. She throws her breasts over her shoulders to escape!). Whatever the truth, a film maker called Will Wright made a short fictional movie called *Wild Hunt* based in Suffolk about a man on a quest to investigate the myths. I am featured in the film, which was premiered at Ipswich Film Theatre on Halloween in 2006. You can also hear a song about Black Shuck on the Lowestoft band The Darkness' album. Unfortunately, they were only able to find one word to rhyme with his name, and it wasn't luck! Great act though. There was also a Border Morris side named after him, who were brilliant, but now sadly disbanded. More recently, I took part in filming a documentary, which was shown on BBC4 in early summer of 2009; *Beowulf & Anglo Saxon Poetry* is presented by Michael Wood, and includes contributions by Dr. Sam Newton, Brian Glover and myself.

Long after my own original researches, I found a wonderful new book on the subject. *Explore Phantom Black Dogs* (Heart of Albion Press, 2005, 152 pages) is edited by Bob Trubshaw, and contains chapters by various authors, including Alby Stone. It is pretty comprehensive, and includes analysis of the psychology of the phenomena as well as the folklore and detailed bibliography. You can obtain it direct from: www.hoap.co.uk (ISBN 1872883788).

The Origins of Beowulf and the Pre-Viking Kingdom of East Anglia
    (Boydell & Brewer, 1993, 182 pages) by Dr. Sam Newton (ISBN 0859914720).

Wild Hunt film by Will 'Rev' Wright (Film Tribe, 2006, 24 minutes), can be seen for free at: www.vimeo.com/2029339

For a wider view of sources of wild hunt legends across Europe and elsewhere see:

The Folklore of the Wild Hunt and the Furious Host by Kveldulf Hagen from Mountain Gundarsson, *Thunder*, Issue #7, winter, 1992. http://www.vinland.org/heathen/mt/wildhunt.html

Pete Jennings' homepages are at: www.gippeswic.demon.co.uk

Borderlands: Fairy and Liminality in the Scottish Lowlands

KEVIN MANWARING

'THE PLACE OF THE FOREIGNER'

I will discuss the cluster of Fairy Lore situated in the Scottish Lowlands, specifically the Borders, and how the geo-political influences there converged in the folkloric.

Firstly though, I must disclose my interest.

I have been a professional storyteller since 2000 and interested in myths and legends long before that, an interest which manifests in my fiction, poetry, and non-fiction. I have collected folk tales for The History Press, and I am currently writing a novel set in the area. So, onwards.

The Lowlands (Scots: the Lallans or the Lawlands; and in Scottish Gaelic: a' Ghalldachd, "the place of the foreigner"), a place not necessarily 'low' (it has its share of mountains) or even a place (it is not an official geographical or administrative area of the country), seems to have more than its fair share of ballads and tales associated with Fairy/Faerie, indeed some of the best known of all. And it is to those we'll turn to first, before looking at folklore and historical factors.

Yet, a caveat.

The Gaelic epithet, 'the place of the foreigner,' is a provocative one: for the Highlanders, it would mean the Scots-speaking Lowlanders; for the native Scots, it would be the Sassenach

English south of the border, whose influence – invited or invaded – crept in. It echoes the names for the Brythonic tribes – the Waleas, the Welsh, the 'strangers over the border' who were ironically here long before those Johnny-come-lately Saxons. Anyone who crosses a border becomes a 'foreigner'. As an Englishman crossing this border, I am aware of my status as an Anglophone interloper – the linguistically-challenged stranger – although sometimes the perspective of the outsider affords a certain clarity.

Yet, as much as possible, I will relate things in the words of those who live there.

BORDER BALLADS

The Scottish Lowlands have an exceptional cluster of supernatural folk ballads – Thomas the Rhymer, Tam O'Shanter, and Tam Lin to name three – some of which, although being geographically specific, have proved to be moveable feasts, traveling across the borders of not only land, but also the sea, reaching as far as North America, Canada and Australia (Child, Sharp, Lomax, et al).

The oral tradition of a region is a long and tangled skein – beyond the scope of this talk to do justice to. Sometimes it is possible to trace a ballad back to the historical event it records – to a particular battle, death of a historic figure, or notorious murder (e.g. the *Child Ballad 161*: 'The Battle of Otterburn' – which took place on the 19th August, 1338). But others prove more elusive to track and mysterious in their origins. How far back they go, who can say? But I would ken that as long as folk have been gathering around fires, there has been the sharing of stories, songs, chants, jokes, and other word-magics. Did the aboriginal Picts make music or weave tales to pass a long winter's night? No doubt, but none have survived that we know of. Their tongues are stone – and they only speak to us in the strange carved crosses they have left behind and the odd outlier word.

Yet their influence might have lingered in other ways – even folk memory.

In Roxburgh, half a mile west of Ednam, there stands a knoll known as the Piper's Grave. A Pictish burial mound which was once called Picts' Knowe. Local people believed it was a fairy hill into which a piper crept, anxious to learn the haunting tunes of the 'little folk'. But the man had foolishly entered without a protective talisman and was never seen again.

In this fragmentary folk tale we have perhaps a clue as to the ontological transmission which might have occurred at such places. Even if we dismiss it as a record of an actual event, it has key motifs which echo throughout the tales of fairy abduction and the transgressive ballads of the region. The aspirant bard crosses a threshold, enters a forbidden place, breaks a taboo and either gains a power – the gift – or is 'taken'.

The Celtic Tradition has several examples of musicians and poets receiving their 'gift', or particular melodies or odes, from supernatural sources – a phenomenon not exclusive to the Pagan. The illuminated manuscript of *The Book of Kells* (c.800AD, Trinity College Dublin, MS 58) was said to be the 'work of angels'. The blind Irish harper Turlough O'Carolan claimed to have received songs from Faerie (e.g. *'Bean Righ Na Sibhrach, The Faery Queen'*). It seems that Fairy – or more specifically, its Queen – acts as an initiatrix and muse figure (a theory Robert Graves explores doggedly in *The White Goddess*, 1948).

As Graves has been accused of, by citing such examples one runs the risk of finding the evidence to fit the theory, or the fairy. Start looking for the 'smoking muse' and you'll see her everywhere. Before long, you end up with the questionable gender stereotype of the femme fatale – Keats' *La Belle Dame Sans Merci*, where the object of desire transmogrifies into one of fear. The idealised muse becomes 'The Cruel Mother' (Child 20).

So, to the ballads themselves.

Let us turn to the most famous encounter between a poet and the Queen of Elfland.

Thomas the Rhymer

The well-known *Border Ballad* of 'Thomas the Rhymer' is attributed to the thirteenth-century Thomas of Ercildoune, a historical but elusive figure who lived in the area of what is now Earlston, Berwickshire. The ballad relates an encounter between 'True Thomas' and the Queen of Elfland. One day (May Eve), while sitting upon Huntley Bank, Thomas beholds an otherworldly woman – richly clad, she rides a fine horse adorned with silver bells. She introduces herself as the Queen of Elfland and summons Thomas to her land, to 'serve her' for seven years. They ride for 40 days and nights through a blood-red liquid until they arrive at a tree whose fruit is forbidden (in some versions, the Queen gives Thomas an apple, which bestows upon him the gift of prophecy). There they have a ritual meal, before the Queen shows Thomas three roads – to Heaven, to Hell, and to Fairyland. They sojourn to the latter, where Thomas resides for the set term. Upon his return, he wears clothes of an elven green.

This crossing of a threshold results in a gift – in Thomas' case, the Tongue that Cannot Lie (the gift of prophecy, which Thomas of Ercildoune was said to have, hence his epithet 'True Thomas': Thomas used his gift of prophecy to foretell many great events in Scotland, like the death of King Alexander III, the Battle of Bannockburn and the union of Scotland and England under a King born of a French Queen). These prophecies are extant and seem to add credence to Thomas' personal creation myth – unless we choose to deconstruct it as an adept bit of early medieval spin-doctoring.

Yet, could this exchange be read as a metaphor for the creative process? Is the otherworldly border-crossing in fact a synaptic leap – the exchange between the left and right sides of the brain?

The encounter was said to have taken place on the Eildon Hills, in the Scottish Borders, which I visited back in the early 90s, conducting my own phenomenological research (I spent a very windy night on the Eildon Hills – it is one of several hills which have an initiatory aspect, e.g. Cader Idris, Snowdonia – where a night spent sleeping there will result in either death, madness or inspiration, or perhaps a combination of all three: a dead, mad poet!).

The Rhymer's Glen (visited by Sir Walter Scott with J.M.W. Turner) and the nearby Rhymer Stone seem to attest to the 'veracity' of the legend – the latter was in fact erected in 1929 by the Melrose Literary Society and supposedly marks the spot on which the fabled Eildon Tree once grew – under which, the historical Thomas was said to have taken his famous nap. A similar plaque at the British Camp, on the Malvern Hills, marks where the medieval poet, William Langland, describes Piers Plowman sitting down and receiving his vision of the 'Great Plain' while he 'slombred on a sleping.'

In Pembrokeshire (formerly Dyfed) is Gorsedd Arberth, a mound at Narberth, where *The Mabinogion* tells us Pwyll, Lord of Dyfed, beheld a similar vision in white – Rhiannon, who initiates him into the deep and perilous mysteries of marriage.

Is there a link between these sites – as hills of initiatory vision? Or is it just a simple topographical fact that from a hill you can see further, and can often feel inspired – the rush of endorphins when reaching the summit conducive to an epiphanic sensation?

Another tradition relates to the 'king sleeping under the hill,' or to a buried treasure – e.g. King Sil, who was believed to have been interred beneath Silbury Hill, Wiltshire (although all archaeological excavations to date have proven to the contrary).

Perhaps then it is not surprising to discover that the Eildon Hills have their own legend of a fool figure (in this case, a fellow named Canonbie Dick) who discovers King Arthur and his knights – and has the power to awaken them with a horn. As is usually the case, the trespasser fails to win the treasure, the royal entourage remains dormant – mythical sleeper agents – and the culprit dies soon after relating his tale.

Could such stories of sleeping kings be a metaphor for our own dormant potential and what might befall us if we fail to activate it? [King Arthur's Cave, actually in the Forest of Dean – there are several around the land – lots of potential!]

FOLKLORE & FOLK TALES

The presence of such memorials (sites of neo-pilgrimage, e.g. Aberfoyle) fixes the legend, and they become a form of 'belief battery', storing up the mythic associations of a place, added to by every subsequent pilgrim.

Other spurious monuments (e.g. the grave of Beddgelert, North Wales) become money-spinning omphaloi, boosting the local tourist economy. In the hills above Aberfoyle, is the home of Rev. Robert Kirk, seventeenth-century Scottish Minister and author of 1691 monograph, *The Secret Commonwealth of Elves, Fauns and Fairies* – signposts bearing red mushrooms lead visitors on the Fairy Trail to the 'fairy circle' which Kirk was said to have stepped in, disappearing into Fairyland where, according to his legend, he remains trapped to this day.

Despite the kitsch quality of this commodified mythscape, some visitors have attested to psychic experiences, even receiving communication from Kirk himself (Stewart, 1990). A form of channelling is said to take place, and wisdom from the 'Otherworld' is downloaded.

Are such experiences a way of creating meaningful narratives for the mysterious process of inspiration?

Sites that have a liminal quality – streams, caves, glades, pools, romantic ruins, shorelines, bridges – and certain times of day (dawn, dusk) and year (midsummer, midwinter, May Eve,

Samhain) have been frequently conducive to creativity, not only featuring in the content of ballads and tales, but creating the conditions for their composition in the first place. The pink noise of, say, a babbling brook, affects the brainwaves, changing them from Alpha to Theta – when greater synaptic leaps occur, the spark of inspiration bridging the gap. Is this the 'fire in the head' W.B. Yeats describes in *The Song of Wandering Aengus*, in which the protagonist goes out to a hazel wood and, at a transitional time, encounters the Muse in the form of a 'glimmering girl', which he spends the rest of his life pursuing?

Time for a fairy story.

The Fairy Boy of Leith

The story of the so-called Fairy Boy of Leith is recorded in Richard Bovet's racily titled 1684 tome, *Pandaemonium Or The Devil's Cloyster*.

It tells of an encounter between a Captain George Burton and an unusual ten-year-old lad who told Burton that every Thursday night he capered off to Calton Hill, near Edinburgh, where he entered through a pair of huge gates, visible only to those who had the fairy gift. At the revels under the hill, he played the drums while the Little Folk danced. 'A great company, both men and women' gathered there to be entertained 'with many sorts of musick' while they feasted and drank. Sometimes they all flew off to France or Holland and back in a night 'to enjoy the pleasures of these countries.' Sometimes 'France' or somewhere equally 'exotic' to a Brit was an analogue for Faerie, hence Shakespeare's setting of that quintessentially English fairy story, *A Midsummer Night's Dream*, in a wood near Athens.

It was said that 'all the people in Scotland' could not keep the Fairy Boy from his Thursday night flitting. So Captain Burton, accompanied by some friends, tried to hold the lad in conversation one night. They placed themselves between the

Fairy Boy and the door of the room in which they were sitting, but about an hour before midnight they suddenly realised that the boy had slipped away unobserved. He was found just as he was about to leave the house and brought back to the room once more. Again, everyone watched him closely but he eluded them, and vanished to keep his nocturnal tryst on Calton Hill.

There are similar stories up and down the land – e.g. the Green Children of Suffolk. Any fairy unfortunate enough to stray into this realm usually doesn't fare well. If we read this story metaphorically, we can see echoes with the other material of the Borders – a fairy hill, a Crossing between this world and another, otherworldly music, threshold guardians preventing a return (in this case, to Faerie), and a vanishing (like Thomas the Rhymer or Robert Kirk).

The fact that this account was published less than a decade before Kirk's manuscript and subsequent disappearance implies the Reverend was no doubt aware of it, and perhaps even inspired by it.

It seems that Fairy Phenomena was in vogue at the time. Did it offer a counternarrative to the Age of Enlightenment, as in the late Victorian Age, when it seemed to be an allergic reaction to the iron cults of the Industrial Revolution?

This speculation leads us to historical factors.

HISTORICAL FACTORS

James VI of Scotland, later James I of England, famously described the Lowlanders in unflattering terms: 'Even from their cradells bredd and brought up in theft, spoyle and bloode.' A hard country bred hard people, as the long and bloody history of the Scottish Borders attests. The harsh reality of existence in a cold, rain-lashed borderland also added to the palimpsest of narratives which saturate the area, providing a rich peat distilled into the tales and ballads preserved for a long time in the oral culture of the area, as well as its literary heritage. With the referendum on Scottish independence looming (2014), narratives of nationhood and the 'hot zones' of disputed territory will become increasingly topical.

Border Reivers

Living on the edge of things can make you vulnerable, and perhaps more prone to articulate your culture and status. It can also make you opportunistic. Border Reivers gave the Lowlands a bad name (and gave the English language such treasures as 'ruffian', 'blackmail', and 'bereaved') and have become interwoven into the fabric of its folklore, although they were very much a real presence. From the late thirteenth century to the beginning of the seventeenth century, these raiders thrived along the Anglo-Scottish border. These mobs recruited from both Scottish and English families, and they fell upon the rich farms of the Border country with impunity, regardless of their victims' nationality. Like a plague of locusts, they swarmed and, while rich pickings and a vacuum of authority lasted, their colonies prospered – they were the unacknowledged kings of the Border for around a century, their reign straddling the Stuart Kings of Scotland and the Tudor Dynasty of England. A modern analogy might be Mexican drug cartels – plundering the cash cow of their rich neighbour – but with the Reivers, it was more smash-and-grab (most commonly cattle, a long and venerable tradition in Celtic legend, as in their Irish forebears and such tales as *The Cattle Raid of Cooley*).

Yet it is hard to romanticise the Border Reivers in the same way that we tend to with Robin Hood, Dick Turpin, or even Blackbeard. It is unlikely the Reivers will receive a glamorous movie makeover. They were, on the whole, a nasty bunch – the notorious Armstrong Gang among the Hall of Infamy of the area. Operating out of Langholm, their awful deeds became the stuff of thrilling local folklore. This corner of Dumfriesshire was convenient for them. From here, they could easily pop over the Border when the moon was right – hence their saying: 'There will be moonlight again.'

Curiously, a descendant of the Armstrong's of Mangerton became the first man on the moon: Neil Armstrong. When he visited the town on his world tour on the 11th March, 1972, he was made the first Freeman of Langholm.

On a metaphorical level, Border Reivers could be seen as the active agents of the imagination – crossing over the divide, making fiery connections, and returning with the contraband of ideas.

Pushing this metaphor further, the raiders also often removed 'in sight', easily portable household goods or valuables, and took prisoners to ransom. A novelist does little less with his plundering of lives and corralling of characters.

The moon has long been perceived as a symbol of dreams, of the unconscious. Armstrong's historic flight was perhaps the ultimate 'border raid' to the terrain of the imagination – firing up a generation with dreams of what could be possible if mankind was daring and ingenious enough.

To return to terra firma – the Border Reivers did not appear out of thin air, but arose out of the push/pull factors of extreme hardship. Caught in the crossfire between the feuding armies of Scotland and England, from the inheritance system of 'gavelkind' (by which estates were divided equally between all a man's sons upon his death, so that many people owned insufficient land to maintain themselves), the unproductive land which made self-sufficiency difficult, the distance from any seat of government, and alternating trends of indulgence and active encouragement, to draconian and indiscriminate punishment – all stoked the fire.

Yet a further blow was to come to the region ...

The Lowland Clearances

The traditional system of agriculture in Lowland Scotland had existed unchanged for hundreds of years. In many ways, it was a totally rural economy, the land being worked by the cottars (part-time labourers/subtenants) on the centuries-old runrig system of subsistence farming – a system of land occupation, the name refers to its characteristic ridge and furrow pattern, with alternating 'runs' (furrows) and 'rigs' (ridges). These ancient agrarian rhythms, shaping the land, were maintained for generations – families of farmers, ploughing their own furrow. The Agricultural Revolution in Scotland devastated all of that – a series of changes in agricultural practice that began in the seventeenth century and continued into the nineteenth century. Modernisation of farming methods was the ostensible agenda – yet the price of productivity was the impact on human lives.

The cottars were brutally replaced with full-time agricultural labourers who lived either on the main farm or in rented accommodation in growing or newly founded villages. Small settlements were torn down; their occupants moved to new, purpose-built villages. Other displaced farmers moved to the new industrial centres of Glasgow, Edinburgh and Northern England. In other areas, such as the southwest, landowners offered low rents and nearby employment to tenants they deemed to be 'respectable'. As farmland became more commercialised, land was often rented through auctions, leading to an inflation of rents that priced many tenants out of the market.

During the Lowland Clearances (as they have become known by Devine, and others), between 1760 and 1830, many Scottish Lowlanders – out of work, or turfed off their land – migrated prior to the American Revolution; and tens of thousands migrated particularly after 1776, taking advantage of the many new opportunities offered in America and Canada to own and farm their own land.

A theory popular in the nineteenth century (Sir Walter Scott's) suggested that the legends of the 'Little People' who lived under the hills were a folk memory of the displacement of early indigenous tribes (e.g. Picts, or Pechs). In Ireland, it was the Tuatha Dé Danaan who were meant to be the original aboriginal aristocracy, subsumed by waves of invasions and by St. Patrick and the Cross – driven into the 'hollow hills'. And yet, in the Lowland and later Highland Clearances (and the Potato Famine in Ireland), you have a very real displacement of people who have had a long connection with a landscape – who 'vanish', leaving the hills empty (clear of forests and farmers, to graze sheep). This, I suggest, fed into the popularity of tales and ballads of the Hidden People on both sides of the Atlantic – by natives, who mourn the loss of their ancestral cousins 'into the west'; and by Irish-Scots migrants, fuelled by the longing of exile from the mother country. On both sides, the romanticisation of the other occurs. Absence makes the heart grow fonder, the imagination more vivid in filling in the gaps, in creating consoling fictions which offer a 'mythic reading' of an event of national trauma.

And in the Fairy Tradition of the Borders we seem to have a mirroring of this historicity. These 'composite creatures' as Kirk called them, 'of a midle Nature betuixt Man and Angel' – exiled from heaven, shut out of hell, forever suspended in a limbo existence – have been both demonised and championed. They are, in some ways, the original asylum seekers. Is this why the belief in them has lingered in these Borderlands, whose populace see a metaphor of their own ambiguous status?

CONCLUSION

The Fairy Tradition of the Scottish Borders seems to be the result of several factors: the rich oral tradition of the region which mixed the voices of the minstrels and the Makars, the stern edicts of the Kirk and the gritty heathenism of the Picts; the cut-and-thrust of historical factors – the Border Reivers, the Lowland Clearances, the changing status of the Scottish Nation; the bedrock of geological and geographical factors; the linguistic streams of English, Lowland Scots, and Gaelic; the dramatic weather and ruin-strewn landscape – all distilled into the singular 'malt' of tales and ballads which linger there yet.

Yet, what do they mean for us?

I propose that the many 'crossing' narratives of the Fairy Tradition offer a metaphor for the creative process – that when artists or writers describe the 'Other', depict 'Otherworlds', and invent its 'exotic' inhabitants, they are merely giving form to their own inner daemons, and articulating the enervating transfusion which occurs when things cross over.

Whenever we go 'inside ourselves' to seek inspiration, we become Thomas the Rhymer or Janet o' Carterhaugh – crossing the threshold, breaking the membrane of taboo, encountering our Higher Self or Shadow, and receiving a transmission. If we are fortunate, or skilled enough – we return with its message, and hope the signal is not broken.

Irish Druidry and the Modern Druid Movement

LUKE EASTWOOD

Most Druids and indeed Pagans generally would be aware that Druids existed in Ireland and fewer I suspect may know that Druidry/Druidism (draíochta in Irish means Druidry, synonymous with magic generally) continued uninterrupted during and after the Roman period that changed the face of Western Europe. The most common and well-known stream of modern Druidry is derived mostly from Welsh sources, rediscovered during the romantic revival; however, the Druidry of Ireland has also had a huge impact on the survival of Druidic knowledge and on the development of the modern movement itself. The Romans swept through Western Europe and, in the process, usurped the existing Celtic culture and their civilisation, beginning with Cisalpine Gaul and culminating with the colonisation of Southern Britain. During this period, the Romans outlawed what we now refer to as Druidry/Druidism and imposed their own religious and social structures, leading to an acceptable middle ground of Romano-Gaulish and Romano-British deities that we know of from archaeology and written records.

The indigenous Celtic culture was assimilated or eliminated in all of Europe except Ireland, Scotland, Wales, and the most western and northern parts of what is now England. Although the Romans had long been aware of Iuverna or Hibernia, any plans to conquer Ireland were never enacted. Of all the countries in

Southern and Central Europe, only Ireland remained completely untouched by Roman purposes of trade or influence; few visited the country, and solely for the reconnaissance.

Likewise, with Roman influence, Ireland was untouched by the Anglo-Saxons and, like Scotland, was late to succumb to the influence of Norman culture and feudalism. The result of this isolation was that the existing Celtic structures of governance, social, economic, and religious life continued much as they had since ancient times. Changes obviously occurred with the passing of time and also as a result of a gradual shift from Paganism to Christianity and the influence of Viking raiding and settlement in both Ireland and Scotland. However, the overriding cultural influence in both countries was that of the Gael, evidenced most clearly by the language (*Gaeilge* and *Gáidhlig* respectively), laws, dress and social structure.

Unfortunately, by the eighteenth century, when the Druid revivalist movement began, the link between mainstream society and Bardic/Druidic culture had been severed, with only a very small number of Irish individuals or triads continuing their ancient traditions in secret. Sadly, the last of the secret Druids who had any recognisable claim to be hereditary seem to have died in the 1990s. Two Irish men I know of (via people who actually met or knew them personally) each claimed to be the last survivors of a different triad – three members: *file* (Bard), *fáith* (Ovate), *druí* (Druid). Neither of these two men had an initiate or acolyte to pass on their knowledge to – so, sadly, whatever secrets they had to tell died with them.

Despite this setback of lost continuity, Ireland was to have a direct influence on the re-emergence of Druidry in Britain. John Toland, credited with founding the Ancient Druid Order (ADO), was born in 1670 and raised in Donegal (North West Ireland) in a Catholic family. After converting to Protestantism at sixteen, he studied at Glasgow and Edinburgh universities before moving to Holland and later England. From the outset of his writing career, he caused controversy leading to attempts by the Irish parliament to have him executed for heresy. As a political and religious maverick, he was considered the first of the freethinkers, writing extensively on religion, history, social and political issues of the day. He claimed himself to be a pantheist, which was quite outrageous at the time, although he wrote only one book on the subject of Druids and Celtic religion – *A Critical History of the Celtic Religion and Learning: Containing an Account of the Druids* (1726). Toland was quite famous in his time but now is completely forgotten outside of academic and Druidic circles.

Despite its Irish founder, the ADO (founded in England, 1717) was largely based on romantic ideas derived from Roman accounts, fantasy and the emerging Welsh remnants of Bardism, especially the dubious work of Iolo Morganwg (Edward Williams). Likewise, the Ancient Order of Druids (AOD, founded 1781) was romantic with a roughly Freemason structure. Other similar groups sprang up in Wales and France, and in USA the Ancient Order of Druids in America began in 1912. It was not until the mid-twentieth century that Irish Druidic remains were brought to light outside of the Celtic Twilight (in Ireland) or the academic circles of Ireland, England, France and Germany. The man responsible for this new awareness of Irish sources and the re-emergence of Gaelic culture into the modern Druid movement was a writer of German and Irish parentage – Robert Graves.

Ironically, Graves was a classicist and novelist, not a Gaelic scholar like his (Irish) father and grandfather (Bishop Charles Graves, member of the Royal Irish Academy and expert on Ogham and Brehon Law). In his 1948 book, *The White Goddess*, he made use of the largely unknown *Song of Amergin* and the Irish Ogham alphabet – both of which date back to the pre-Christian period of Ireland.

Graves' scholarship and theories were in part based on false premises and poorly researched, second-hand information, leading to intense criticism of the book; in particular due to his ignorance of his own paternal family's sound academic knowledge of Irish materials. Despite his fanciful shortcomings, it should be acknowledged that Robert Graves single-handedly reintroduced Irish Druidic sources to the mainstream of alternative spirituality and the Druid movement that had largely forgotten their existence.

It was Ross Nichols (along with Gerald Gardner) who introduced the eightfold festival celebrations often referred to as the 'Wheel of the Year'. Ross used Welsh names for the astronomical solar festivals of the solstices and equinoxes, but he used the Irish names, derived from the ancient Irish Pagan festivals, for the four remaining festivals. Modern archaeological research and examination of ancient written sources and folk survivals clearly demonstrate that all eight festivals were celebrated in Ireland, if not elsewhere. The dates and practices of the modern festivals may not tally with those celebrated by the ancient Irish Druids; however, prior to Nichols' innovations, there was no official recognition of these seasonal events across the Druidic world.

Since that time, the OBOD and other modern orders, such as Ár nDraíocht Féin (ADF), BDO, Henge of Keltria, Druid Clan of Dana, and Ord na Druí have all embraced Irish Celtic sources, the eight festivals and Irish language to varying degrees.

Thanks to many translations from Gaeilge of the eighteenth, nineteenth and early twentieth centuries, the surviving mythology, Brehon Law, poetry, place history (Dindshenchas), cosmology, Ogham alphabet, tree and plant lore, etc. has not only been preserved for the modern reader, but has provided a contemporaneous non-classical source for the modern Druid movement.

During the Elizabethan era, spoken and written Gaeilge (Irish language) was outlawed on pain of death. Many ancient Irish books were found and burnt, but some made their way to English aristocratic collections or museums. Many books were hidden, by the Irish, under floors or in walls, in order to escape destruction by the English colonists. Of course, many manuscripts were forever lost, forgotten or destroyed, but fortunately many did survive in ecclesiastic institutions (in Ireland and Europe) and among the aristocracy until the prohibition was lifted.

Academics began translating from ancient and medieval Irish into modern English, French or German from the eighteenth century onwards – notable people we have to thank for this great legacy are Kuno Meyer, Whitely Stokes, R.A.S. MacAlister, P.W. Joyce, Eugene O'Curry, and Augusta Gregory, to name but a few.

Without the pioneering work of these translators, the annals and works of the ancient and medieval Irish, that preserved much of what we now know about Druidic culture, would probably still be unknown and gathering dust in the world's museums and university vaults.

Indeed, a new wave of Pagan authors, such as Caitlín and John Matthews, R.J. Stewart, Alexi Kondratiev, and Koch & Carey, etc., have continued this exploration of the forgotten Irish, Scottish and Welsh translations, much to the enrichment of modern Druidry and our understanding of the Celts in general.

Sadly, what has been unearthed and translated is merely scratching the surface of what remains untranslated in university and museum archives. One can only wonder what gems lie waiting to be discovered? Unfortunately, as Irish Celtic scholar Daragh Smyth explained to me, the process of translating these texts into modern languages is highly specialised, slow, labour-intensive and hence very expensive.

New translations and occasional new texts of Celtic source material do make it to publication from time to time (e.g. via C.E.L.T.), but there does not seem to be any organised programme or major investment in the process. Most ungratifying for myself and others is the fact that exploration of the Celtic texts seems to be confined to the world of academia with little or no access provided for the Druid or wider Pagan community. The academic world is generally not concerned with our religious or cultural practices, except from a historical or anthropological viewpoint – so perhaps it is no surprise that some modern Pagans' desire for new verifiable sources is not taken seriously.

I am hopeful that this attitude might change in the future, regarding Irish sources and indeed with regard to all ancient texts that remain untranslated. Given the re-emergence of Paganism and its new-found legal status, I will enable lobbying for the situation to change The breadth of ancient Celtic thought and practice is only being fully revealed to modern Pagans now in this twenty-first century, long after the re-emergence of the Druids. It is an exciting prospect for the future, especially now that Paganism is no longer illegal or disreputable. As I do with Paganism generally, I look forward to seeing Druidry evolve and continue to rediscover its ancient origins.

Luke Eastwood is a member of Irish and International Druid orders; he co-founded irishdruidnetwork.org and facilitates a Druid grove in Co. Wexford, Ireland. He is also the author of *The Druid's Primer* and *The Journey*, both published by Moon Books. You can read more of his work at: lukeeastwood.com

Isles of the Dead

KEVIN MAINWARING

Where do we go when we die? This question has haunted humankind for millennia and although no firm proof has come to light, there is no shortage of theories! This article attempts to make a minor foray into this nebula of super-abundant speculation, on a raid in the spirit of King Arthur's – as recorded in Taliesin's poem, *Preiddeu Annwn* (where the Pendragon wins the fabled Cauldron of Plenty from the Underworld). We will focus on two grails here: isles of the dead and islands of the ever-living – which often overlap like a vesica piscis – and it is perhaps only in that 'space between', that mandorla, that such places can ultimately be found: in the liminal cracks of knowledge and in a 'between' state of mind.

There's a plethora of lost islands, as I explore in my book of that name, but here the focus will be on funerary islands. So, in the words of Pope John-Paul-George-and-Ringo: 'turn off your mind, relax and float downstream …' as we voyage to the isles of the deceased and the deathless.

There are many islands of the dead, both actual and mythical, although by their very nature, the former overlap with the latter: they have an otherworldly nature by design. They are meant to serve as an interface between the quick and the dead: a terminal to life's journey; an entrepôt to the deadlands. Here we'll look at a few examples, scattered around the British Isles and beyond; with the awareness that we enter treacherous waters: for where one ends and the other begins is hard to gauge. Real funerary islands have a mythic atmosphere, and mythical isles of the dead blur into islands of the ever-living: mortality becomes immortality.

Cintra Pemberton, in *Soulfaring*, says: "Islands to the west, lying in the path of the setting sun, figure strongly in Celtic legends and myths, where they are usually seen to be dwelling places of the blessed dead."

T.W. Rolleston, in his classic *Celtic Myths and Legends*, describes how the whole of Great Britain itself was perceived as a Land of the Dead to the Classical World:

> "According to an unknown writer cited by Plutarch, who died about the year 120 of the present era, and also by Procopius, who wrote in the sixth century A.D., the Land of the Dead is the western extremity of Great Britain, separated from the eastern by an impassable wall. On the northern coast of Gaul, says the legend, is a populace of mariners whose business is to carry the dead across from the continent to their last abode in the island of Britain. The mariners, awakened in the night by the whisperings of some mysterious voice, arise and go down to the shore, where they find ships awaiting them which are not their own, and, in these, invisible beings, under whose weight the vessels sink almost to the gunwales. They go on board, and with a single stroke of the oar, says one text, in one hour, says another, they arrive at their destination, though with their own vessels, aided by sails, it would have taken them at least a day and a night to reach the coast of Britain. When they come to the other shore, the invisible passengers land, and at the same time the unloaded ships are seen to rise above the waves, and a voice is heard announcing the names of the new arrivals, who have just been added to the inhabitants of the Land of the Dead."

Manx fisherman offered this prayer to the sea as they put off from Manannan's eponymous isle:

Manannan beg Mac y Lir,
Little Manannan, son of the sea,
Who blessed our island,
Bless us and our boat, going out well,
Coming back better with both living and dead aboard.

This could have just referred to their catch, but seems to have a psychopompic or placatory function too.

Bardsey Island, off the tip of the Llyn Peninsula, Wales, is reputed to be the Isle of Twenty Thousand Saints. One of its appellations is Bangor Gadfan, after St. Cadfan, who colonised it in 516 CE. His successor, St. Lleuddad ab Dingad, was visited by an angel who granted him requests. One of them was that the soul of anyone buried on the island should not go to hell. This was apparently granted and Bardsey became des res for the dead! The twelfth-century poet Meilir prayed in his "Death-bed of the Bard" that he might be buried there. Its Welsh name is Ynys Enlli – three trips to Bardsey was the equivalent of one trip to Rome, in the medieval form of carbon credits, pilgrim points or God's air miles. It lies at the end of a western pilgrimage route like Santiago de Compostela, dotted with water-chapels, such as St. Cybi's Well, to refresh the thirsty and foot-sore pilgrims.

Yet some islands are surprisingly close. In Kent, there lies Thanet, literally 'the dead isle' (from the Latin for death, thanatos). Bernard Cornwell, in *The Winter King*, describes what John Cowper Powys called the Isle of Slingers (Portland in Dorset) as serving the same function: a Dark Age isle of the dead or damned; and to this day, its ugly rock-breaking penal colony atmosphere gives it still the same blighted ambience – a gobbet of gritty phlegm at the end of the longest spit in the world, Chesil Beach.

In a nod to her mythic name and fate, the late Princess Diana was said to have been laid to rest on an island in a lake at Althorpe

– the Spencer estate, near Northampton. However, this seems to have been a ruse to throw morbid tourists and potential grave robbers off the scent. She was apparently laid to rest in the family vault at the nearby church, St John's, Little Brington. The watery memorial in Hyde Park was an allusion to this 'Isle of Diana', one that was widely accessible to tourists, similarly diverting them from her actual resting place. The memorial's flowing design was intended to 'reflect Diana's life' and symbolise 'her and openness' (www.royalparks.org.uk accessed 20/07/07). Both are modern examples of 'isles of the dead', illustrating the mythic power such places have. Such islands are cut-off from everyday life – we can visit them to pay our respects and then gratefully return.

The burial of royalty on islands, real or otherwise, is not unprecedented. The burial place of Pictish kings is the Isle of Lismore, off the Benderlock Coast. Pennick tells us that Lismore in Gaelic means 'great garden' – a 'poetic kenning for the otherworldly garden-island of Avalon' (Pennick, p112).

Iona, renowned as a royal burial site, rightfully claims this title, housing the remains of 48 Scottish kings, along with French and Norwegian monarchs, for a total of 60 royal interments. Macduff, referring to Iona, in Shakespeare's *Macbeth*, described it as: 'The sacred storehouse of his predecessors, and guardians of their bones.'

Pennick describes the Isles of the Blest et al in *Celtic Belief* as a third way between heaven and hell (as in 'the bonny road' of Thomas the Rhymer – the way to 'fair Elfland'):

> 'This timeless island paradise lies somewhere to the west in the ocean. At death, one 'goes west'. Celtic burial islands predominantly lie to the west of the land of the living. Only by means of the ship of the dead can the deceased person be brought there. Important people were buried by the shore in the ship that carried them across the sea, enabling them to travel onwards in the world of the dead' (Pennick, p111).

King Arthur famously goes to the Isle of Avalon to 'heal me of my grievous wounds' as immortalised by Tennyson in *Morte d'Arthur* and captured by numerous artists. The Isles of Scilly, called by some the Fortunate Isles, lay claim to not one but two graves of Arthur!

The Viking ship burial at Balladoole, Chapel Hill, Isle of Man, is a classic example of how this common eschatology – the voyage to the Otherworld aboard a boat – crops up again and again in world mythology: Gilgamesh journeys to meet Utnapishtim and his wife (the survivors of the great flood) aboard a boat bearing two poles – which dissolve each time he punts, so he needs one for the return journey. This is mirrored in the tradition of two coins placed over the eyes of the deceased to pay the ferryman of the dead, Charon, whose lot is to convey souls recently born into death across the River Styx.

At Sutton Hoo, we have another famous example: an actual ship buried beneath a mound, stacked with grave goods.

Two otherworldly rivers are crossed by the shaman of the Salish People from what is now Washington State, North West USA, who uses spirit-canoes to retrieve lost souls in the sbeteda'q ceremony. Using song and sacred paddles, and two parallel rows of men to act as crew for the two canoes needed for the rescue mission, the medicine man 'captain' hazards a journey to the Land of the Dead. This afterlife realm is situated, like so many, in the west. There, everything is reversed:

> '... the seasons and also the times of the day in the Land of the Dead are exactly opposite to what they are in this world. When it is midwinter here, it is midsummer there, and when it is night here, it is daytime there' (Haeberlin).

Similar 'death-canoes' that the author visited in the Northern Philippines were made of stone. These were located in caves connected to an underground river system which floods abruptly, as it did when the author traversed it, narrowly missed being washed away!

Such places are reminiscent of Coleridge's *Kubla Khan* – the laudanum-fuelled reverie which is set in the otherworldly analogue, Xanadu: '… where Alph, the sacred river, ran. Through caverns measureless to man, down to a sunless sea …' Coleridge walked on the Mendip Hills with his fellow poet, Robert Southey, and may have been thinking of Wookey Hole, with its river-carved caverns. H.G. Wells spent some time in Wookey and was inspired by the caverns while writing his classic, *The Time Machine* – perhaps he imagined the original Mesolithic dwellers as Morlocks. The hills above Wookey are littered with Bronze Age round-barrows and seem to have been considered, based upon this evidence, as hills of the dead. Coming from the Southwest across an inundated Somerset Levels, the effect would not have been dissimilar to Böcklin's painting. Here was the Island of the Dead: the monument-littered landscape of Britain – an open mortuary house.

There is the possibility that these caves, at Wookey, are the entrance to Annwn – rather than Glastonbury Tor – a far more convincing abode for Gwyn ap Nudd, the West Country's version of Hades or Pluto. Another source, *Vita Merlini* (the Life of Merlin), cites Aquae Sulis (modern-day Bath) as the portal to Avalon – not Glastonbury – and with its hot springs caused by a 4km fault in the Earth, echoed by its name (Aquae Sulis: 'waters of the gap', according to R.J. Stewart), there is perhaps some sense in this.

Certainly, a sea-faring ship could have made it up the Avon as far as Pulteney Weir (built over a natural shift in the river's level), where sea-borne travellers could have alighted to approach the sacred springs – second only to Delphi in the Classical World, with their own Pythia, seer-priestesses, uttering their gnomic prophecies from their fume-filled scrying chambers. A place to glimpse behind the veil.

Author Robert Holdstock charts the unknown regions of the ancestors in his haunting novels. In his *Merlin Codex*, it is Jason's ship the Argo which acts as a funerary barge – filled with sinister sentience: 'She will not be my coffin, she will be the vessel that takes me to the grave.'

The stone ship of Balladoole is aligned with both Snaefell (the white peak at Man's heart, literally 'snow mountain') and the setting sun. This seems to be a common belief – the soul went west at death, towards the setting sun – perhaps in the hope it would be reborn. Nigel Pennick, in *Celtic Sacred Landscapes*, echoes this:

> 'West is the direction in which the sun sets beneath the earth, symbolising the end of the life cycle, and the place to which souls must go before being reborn into another life.'

The reliable way the sun sets and is reborn again has reassured those concerned with death since the dawn of human time. It is seen in many cultures as a sign of the soul's rebirth. Also, on a very practical level: as sun-life. Without it, the world descends into darkness, coldness and, eventually, death. The world would not live without the sun, and every night, in a small way, and every winter, in a greater way, we are reminded of that fact. With dawn, and with the winter solstice, all things are made good again. The night is defeated, for now.

In Egyptian mythology, Osiris, in his boat of a million years, travels through the body of Night (Nut) each night, to be reborn resplendent every day (Ra), foreshadowing the perilous journey that the soul must undertake at the point of death – passing gates of trials, of soul-winnowing – if it is to return to the Source.

Psychopompic funeral ballads like *The Lyke Wake Dirge* provide not only sonic portals for exiting souls, but also a clear geography of the Afterlands – the Whinny Muir, the Brig o'Dread – for the soul to be tested by and to remember ... Island-states to pass through which, perhaps, actual death-islands provide an earthly analogue for.

On a practical level, it makes sense to bury the dead on an island – especially plague victims, so that any infection cannot spread to the mainland. The consecrated parameters of a cemetery separate it from the mundane, and an island goes one step further. Water is said to be a barrier of psychic protection, but perhaps such islands protect the quick from the dead, preventing the fatal infection of death – a form of quarantine. Few cultures live amongst their dead.

Lewis Bonfire Night Celebrations

MARION PEARCE

It is cold, autumn is here, and winter is coming. Many early Pagan festivals are hidden, subsumed into the later Christian world. The best-known date in the calendar in the autumnal days leading up to Yule is November 5th – Guy Fawkes Night or Bonfire Night. In the ancient Pagan Celtic world, bonfires were held to celebrate Samhain on the last night of October, and many of the features of Bonfire Night hint at the earlier celebrations of Samhain.

It is in Lewes, Sussex, where there is held the most dramatic celebrations. Here there are flaming street processions, young men with flaring torches, loud fire crackers, bangers and jumping squibs, people dressed in elaborate fancy dress, tar barrels sent rolling ablaze down the street, and massive bonfires, ten or twelve feet tall. It is literally an explosive night.

The Lewes bonfire celebrations were traditionally anti-Catholic. In the days of Mary Tudor, seventeen Protestant martyrs were burnt to death. Anti-popery sentiments overlaid the festivities; effigies of the Pope were burnt, mock 'bishops' in surplice and gown delivered inflammatory speeches denouncing popery.

Their own version of the traditional Guy Fawkes verse was chanted:

Remember, remember, *the fifth of November, gunpowder, treason and plot;*
I see no reason why gunpowder treason, ever should be forgot.
Guy Fawkes, Guy, 'twas his intent
To blow up the King and the Parliament;
Three score barrels he laid below
To prove old England's overthrow.
By God's Providence he was catched
With a dark lantern and lighted match.
Holla, boys, holla, boys, make the bells ring!
Holla, boys, holla boys, God save the King!
A farthing loaf to feed old Pope
A pennorth o' cheese to choke him,
A pint o' beer to wash it down,
And a faggot o' wood to burn him!
Burn him in a tub o' tar;
Burn him like a blazing star,
Burn his body from his head,
And then we'll say old Pope is dead!
Hip, hip, hooray!

Celebrants of Sussex Bonfire Night were called 'Bonfire Boys'. They could be very rowdy, and often things got out of control. In 1838, there were several arrests, and three years later, in 1841, over twenty people were imprisoned when their riotous behaviour ended in fights with specially sworn in special constables. The magistrate at the following assizes handed out sentences of terms of up to two months for the riotous Bonfire Boys of Lewis.

Unfortunately, this did not stop the antics of the Lewis Bonfire Boys. In 1846, the Lewes magistrate Mr Blackman J.P. went outside his house to try to calm the crowd. They amassed outside his home with tar barrels, which they lighted. Mr Blackman was jeered, then set upon, and rendered senseless when he tried to take the ringleaders into custody.

Earnest debate raged in the local press: should the celebrations be curtailed? The next year, in 1847, the local law enforcement officers got tough. Police were draughted in from as far as London, and over 170 specials, made up of principal local tradesmen, were sworn in to keep the peace. Lord Chichester addressed the crowds from the steps of County Hall, appealing for order – all to no avail, and in desperation he read the Riot Act, for the crowd to disperse. Although the streets were eventually cleared, many of the Metropolitan Police were injured.

Eventually the riots stopped, and the Bonfire Celebrations became more peaceful. Official Bonfire societies were formed which, even today, organise the event. Safety elements were introduced. The famous firework, the Lewes Rouser, which could climb up the side of a house and disappear over its roof, was banned in 1904. Although it was still said that you wore your oldest clothes on Guy Fawkes Day in Lewes, and there was a roaring trade in goggles.

Today there are seven different bonfire societies in Lewes, each with their own costumes, ranging from Tudors to Mongol warriors, and their own route weaving through the town. The Cliffe Bonfire Society was formed in 1853, and they dress as Vikings and Moors. The Commercial Square Bonfire Society was formed in 1855, and dress as Native American Indians and American Civil War soldiers. The Lewes Borough Bonfire Society was formed in 1853, and dress as Zulu warriors and Tudor ladies and gentlemen. Nevill Juvenile, the only children's bonfire society, was formed in 1967, and they dress in the manner of Valencians and mediaeval folk. Southover was recently reformed in 2005, and dress as priory monks and buccaneers. South Street was founded in 1913, and dress as English Civil War soldiers and Siamese dancers. Waterloo was reformed in 1964, and they dress as from the Mongolian Empire, and the Greek and Roman eras. It is certainly a colourful sight when they all amass and congregate, each in their own areas throughout Lewes.

LEWIS BONFIRE NIGHT CELEBRATIONS

It is in Sussex that this fiery festival really explodes. Over 150,000 people visited Lewis in 2003 to see their unique pyrotechnic displays. Normally-sane stockbrokers, solicitors, and carpet salesmen all lose their inhibitions and transform into torch-bearing pyromaniacs, charging around like fire ants. Here is a description of modern-day Lewes from the *Financial Times* published on the 5th November, 2005:

> "On the night itself, the societies march through the steep streets of Lewes carrying paraffin-soaked torches and crosses, and parading effigies of Guy Fawkes, the Pope of 1605, and other 'enemies of the bonfire'. The marchers wear fabulous costumes, Vikings, Zulus, Elizabethans, Red Indians, and are trailed by noisy marching bands. Bonfire Boys run with burning tar barrels to Cliffe Bridge, where they toss them, flaming, into the River Ouse. Later, the societies reconvene at sites around the town to light mountainous bonfires. Members dressed as bishops conduct bonfire prayers and repeatedly ask the crowd: 'What'll we do with him?' The answer, of course, is 'Burn him!' – at which point, the Pope and Guy Fawkes go up in flames and the firework displays begin."

Indeed, not only Guy Fawkes was burnt, but modern political figures were also placed on the bonfire right up until 2005, when the practice was made illegal. In 2001, an effigy of Osama Bin Laden was burnt. Here is a description from the 2005 Lewis Bonfire Night taken from www.blather.net which builds a wonderful picture of this atmospheric celebration, complete with effigy of the then-Home Secretary, John Prescott:

> "The Cliffe Bonfire had a garden shed on the top, covered in slogans, and alongside were massive effigies of the Home Secretary (with an 'I.D.' stamp in his hand, poised to stamp

someone's backside), the Pope and the Gunpowder Plot conspirators – all of which were, well, blown up completely using fireworks launched from inside the sculptures.

While this was going on, three men dressed as an archbishop and bishops stood on a platform, surrounded by flaming crucifixes, while the crowd launched fireworks at them. These men, presumably, were volunteers – or they had done terrible, terrible things. They stood there for a good half-hour, almost being set on fire.

After the chaos had died down and people had sat by the fire for a while, it was time for the late parade – where the members of the bonfire societies can go crazy on the streets, now that those of a gentler disposition have left Lewes. Some of them had earplugs in, and crackers were going off around our feet, and the streets were full of orange paper from inside the bangers. We left at 1:30am, and the noises and flames were only showing the barest signs of abating."

Seriously Modern Dragons: More than a Myth

LUCYA STARZA

At Seriously Monstrous – a conference on cryptozoology – one of the talks was called *Dragons: More than a Myth?* by Richard Freeman.

Richard Freeman is a full-time cryptozoologist – which means he is an expert on monsters and fabulous beasts (and often where to find them). The former zookeeper is also the author of *Dragons: More than a Myth?* and *Explore Dragons*, so he really knows what he is talking about. Here are the notes I took during his lecture:

Dragons are the grandfather of all monsters. They are in the most ancient legends of the human race and can be traced by folklorists back to Africa, before our ancestors left that continent.

As Richard said: "The dragon has his claws deep in the psyche of humanity and is not about to let go."

WESTERN DRAGONS

The Western dragon is a reptile with four legs and breathes fire. They are gods or the enemies of gods in early tales and are only later depicted as being mortal creatures. In Western myths and legends, they are usually evil and often have special powers.

Wyverns are similar to dragons but have two legs and are smaller and less smart. The wyrm is also common in tales across

Europe and Scandinavia. It is limbless, spits poison and, if cut up, the pieces rejoin.

The basilisk is another similar fabulous beast. It is supposedly hatched from a cockerel's egg and incubated by a toad or snake. Looking into a basilisk's eye meant death. It was defeated by showing it its own reflection – or the sound of a cockerel crowing at dawn. A bit like a basilisk, the cockatrice looks bird-like and has a deadly gaze.

EASTERN DRAGONS

In the Orient, dragons are associated with water rather than fire. Chinese dragons have four legs. They do breathe fire, but it condenses and turns to rain. They are usually benevolent. They start life as snakes but grow enormous over centuries, also growing wings.

The katsu is a Japanese dragon. It has three claws and grows more quickly. It is generally benevolent. The naga is from Asia. In India, the naga is depicted as half-human, but originally nagas were giant serpents.

The Persian dragon is a hybrid of Eastern and Western types. It looks Eastern, but breathes fire and is evil.

WHAT LIES BEHIND TALES OF DRAGONS?

In China, dragons are said to shed their bones as well as their skin – although, of course, what are found are dinosaur bones. These bones were thought to have magical and medical powers.

However, there are stories of people interacting with dragons – which is odd if the dinosaurs died out before humans evolved, and if all humans ever found were bones.

WHAT LIVING ANIMAL COULD HAVE INSPIRED TALES OF DRAGONS?

The saltwater crocodile is the biggest living reptile. So, colossal crocodiles could be the answer. They kill large animals. Coins are thrown to appease crocodiles in some cultures, which could explain stories of dragons' hoards of gold.

The largest known lizard is the Komodo dragon. It is venomous and gives a festering bite, then waits for its prey to die.

These had prehistoric ancestors that were much larger, and there are still stories of giant lizards being sighted. In New Guinea there are stories of fire-breathing giant lizards in modern times, although the fire is actually their red tongues. However, they are still very large.

The reticulated python is huge – a 33ft-long python was recorded in the 1930s. Another giant snake is the green anaconda. It is much bulkier than the python. Giant reptiles today are all tropical, but some could perhaps have been brought to the West in menageries.

A book in the 1970s called *The Flight of Dragons* suggested that ancient reptiles might have been like dirigibles filled with hydrogen that could have breathed fire.

THE GLOBAL MONSTER TEMPLATE

This is the idea that there is a template of monsters in the human psyche, because similar monsters are found in tales all over the world. The global monster template includes fairy folk, demonic dogs, phantom cats, and the king of all monsters: dragons.

The templates are distorted analogues of what preyed upon or competed with the ancestors of Homo sapiens – big crocodiles and other giant animals. So, we still have fears deep in our psyche.

But, there could be more to it than just resurfacing fears. The Tibetans believe in 'tulpas' – artificial ghosts. People can create visible tulpas from their thoughts. Maybe our minds are creating tulpas of ancient fears, such as monsters. Another theory put forward by some is that dragons could be creatures from another dimension.

The Occult War: Secret Agents, Magicians and Hitler

MICHAEL HOWARD

It is surprising the number of practitioners of the magical arts and witchcraft who were involved in military and intelligence work during the Second World War. Perhaps the best known 'occult spy' operating in WWII (and, in fact, long before), and whose intelligence career has been well documented, is Aleister Crowley. Author Dr. Richard B. Spence believes that Crowley began his journey to being a secret agent when he took an oath of allegiance to the British Crown. This was at the Malvern College boarding school in 1891, when he joined the cadet corps of the local Worcestershire Royal Artillery Volunteers. Later in life, Crowley was to say that, despite his problems and issues with the British establishment, he had always felt that he was bound to that oath. In fact, it had strengthened his link with England (Spence, 2008, p17). It is possible that he meant on a magical and psychic level, as well as the physical and patriotic one.

As a young man, through an introduction by his aunt, who was a member, Crowley joined the Primrose League. This was a semi-secret, quasi-Masonic, right-wing group within the Conservative Party whose aim was to protect it from its political enemies. Dr. Spence suggests that Crowley's Jacobite sympathies in support of the return of the Stuart dynasty to the British throne, to replace the Hanoverian usurpers, could have been used by the League to persuade Crowley to spy on potential enemies of the Crown. This, however, would suggest that his Jacobite inclinations were not genuine, or merely a passing teenage phase.

Crowley was lucky enough to come under the patronage of the Marquess of Salisbury, the Grand Master of the League. It has been suggested that Salisbury helped Crowley to enter Cambridge University and was grooming his young protégé for a lifelong career in the Diplomatic Service, which might well have involved spying for his country. However, Crowley had other ideas, although it was at Cambridge that he met the future artist Gerald Kelly, and later married his sister, Rose. Forty years or so later, both men were to serve in the wartime British Secret Service (ibid., pp.18–9).

In the First World War, Crowley was living in New York and he was accosted by a stranger on an omnibus. During their conversation about the war in Europe, the man handed Crowley a business card. Printed on it were the addresses of two pro-German magazines, and subsequently Crowley wrote anti-British propaganda for these publications. Naturally the British government took a dim view of this anti-patriotic, traitorous act. They labelled him a traitor and the police raided his magical temple in London and closed it down. Crowley always protested his innocence. In fact, he said he had been working for British Intelligence and written the satirical articles at their request. The aim was to ridicule the pro-German movement in America and discredit the magazines. This has never been confirmed by the British government, but it has also not been denied.

While Crowley was in the States, he also posed as an Irishman supporting home rule or self-government for Ireland, which was still part of the British Empire. He managed to make contact with several Irish-American republicans who shared his alleged views. They seemed to have supplied him with the funds to stay in the country, although they eventually got fed up with his financial demands. It is quite possible that Crowley was spying on the Irish republicans and was sending the information he gleaned back to his handler or case officer in London.

In the early 1920s, Crowley and his little band of followers were expelled from Italy on the direct orders of the fascist dictator, Benito Mussolini. The official version was that they were kicked out because of their 'obscene and perverted' sexual activities at the so-called 'Abbey of Thelema' at Cefalu on Sicily. The real reason was that the Italian police had a secret dossier on Crowley and believed he was a British spy (Spence, 2008, p188).

Rumours circulating in government circles and the media in both Germany and France claimed that Crowley had contacts with 'the intelligence services of foreign countries.' In 1929, he was thrown out of Paris by the French government because they were convinced he was a spy. Dr. Spence believes that at that time Crowley's British Intelligence case officer and contact was Gerald Yorke, who he had met in 1927. Yorke was a freelance journalist and also worked for the international Reuters press agency (ibid., pp.208–9). That could have been a good cover for intelligence activities, and many journalists are still recruited for that purpose today.

In the 1930s, there is the first solid evidence that Crowley was recruited by MI6 or the SIS (Secret Intelligence Service). This was to spy on German occultists with political links to the emerging National Socialist ('Nazi') Party and Marxist revolutionaries. One of Crowley's possible targets was Albert Karl Theodor Reuss, the founder of the magical group the Ordo Templi Orientis (OTO) or Order of the Eastern Templars into which Crowley had been initiated in 1912 and made head of the British branch. Reuss was reputed to have worked before the First World War as an undercover agent for the Prussian secret police. While he was living in London in 1885, Reuss joined the Revolutionary Socialist League run by the founder of the arts and crafts movement, William Morris, and Karl Marx's daughter, Eleanor. When they eventually discovered he was spying on them, Reuss was expelled.

Another prominent member of the OTO in Germany and, controversially, later to become its Grand Master based in the USA, was Karl Johannes Germer. He had been awarded the much-coveted Iron Cross medal in the First World War for his intelligence work, although unfortunately he was imprisoned in a concentration camp by the Nazis. It has been claimed that this was because of his association with Crowley and his attempts to recruit German members for the OTO.

When he was living in Berlin in the 1930s, Crowley spied on secret societies and members of the Nazi Party known to be interested in occultism and reviving the old Germanic Pagan religions. He shared a flat with Gerald Hamilton, a pro-communist English journalist, who was known to British Intelligence as a spy working for the Germans. Crowley reported back to London on Hamilton's activities and no doubt he was doing the same to his German masters. It may have been Crowley's involvement with the SIS that led Heinrich Himmler, head of the Nazi's SS Order, to publicly claim that the British Secret Service was run by Rosicrucians who used their occult powers to spy on their enemies.

In 1933, the year that the Nazis took power in Germany, Crowley met an eccentric Welsh aristocrat named Viscount Tredegar (Evan Morgan 1893–1949). His haunted country house was near Newport in South Wales and was the site of famous wild parties, to which he invited a wide mix of social types including Aldous Huxley and H.G. Wells. The estate included a private zoo featuring a kangaroo, honey bear, baboon and a macaw parrot. Queen Mary, the present queen's grandmother, called Lord Tredegar 'my favourite bohemian'. One of his more unusual and notorious house guests was (perhaps significantly, in light of later dramatic events) the Nazi deputy fuehrer, Rudolf Hess. In fact,

Hess had a family connection with the Tredegar estate, as his first wife was buried nearby. In 2012, the house will be taken over by the National Trust and opened to the public.

Lord Tredegar had also visited the German home of Ernst Rohm, the head of the SA, and they shared a male lover. Rohm, who consulted astrologers about his homosexuality, was assassinated on the orders of Adolf Hitler during the purge of the Nazi Party, known as the 'Night of the Long Knives' in June 1943, when the SA was disbanded. This was partly because Hitler feared the organisation and Rohm's growing power, but also because many of its members shared their leader's sexual preferences and the other top Nazis were homophobes. Crowley's friendship with Lord Tredegar was largely based on the fact that the two men shared an interest in the occult, and possibly because they were both bisexuals. The Great Beast gave his lordship the ultimate accolade of calling him 'the [magical] Adept of Adepts'. Although Tredegar had converted as a young man to Catholicism, and even served as a chamberlain to two popes and was a Knight of Malta, he had still continued his occult activities. While living in Rome, it is said that he performed a necromantic rite in the English Protestant cemetery in the city to conjure up the spirit of the eighteenth-century romantic poet, Shelley. He also had contact with a cunning man in North Wales.

Tredegar seems to have been fond of graveyards for rituals, as he allegedly used the one at the parish church of Ovingdean in Sussex. This was conveniently near his mother's house. In one of these churchyard rituals, he was joined by a group of occultists who included a male cousin of Sir Winston Churchill. Lord Tredegar belonged to an occult secret society in London called The Black Circle, which had the traditional thirteen members of a witch coven. In the Circle, the aristocrat was known as the 'Black Monk' and was even painted in the hooded black robe all the members wore for their ceremonies. He owned several saints' relics, reflecting his Catholic background, had the skeleton of a local Welsh witch set up in his hallway to greet his guests, and confided in Crowley that his family was descended from King Arthur. The legendary city of Camelot was supposed to have been at the nearby Roman site of Caerleon. Crowley even described his lordship as 'the rightful heir to Excalibur'.

When Britain declared war on Germany in September 1939, despite his occult beliefs or possibly because of his unusual connection with Churchill, Lord Tredegar was recruited by MI5 (the internal British Security Service). It is even possible that he belonged to it before the war and was passing information about his Nazi contacts on to Five. He was appointed as the head of the MI6 section known as the Radio Security Service (RSS). Among his other duties in that position, he was in charge of the carrier pigeons used to communicate with secret agents in Nazi occupied Europe.

Unfortunately, his secret career ended abruptly. One day, Tredegar gave an unauthorised office tour to a pretty young woman who did not have security clearance. He was arrested and charged with treason, which was a very serious offence during wartime. It could mean a lengthy time in the Tower of London or even execution by hanging or firing squad. However, to the surprise of his colleagues, the aristocrat was released and it was whispered that MI5 had intervened in the case. Perhaps he knew where too many of the bodies were buried! Immediately, Tredegar contacted his old friend Crowley and tried to persuade him to put a curse on the arresting officer (Spence, 2008, p225, and personal communications from Paul Busby, 13/10/2009).

Another link between Crowley and the intelligence services was his friendship with the homosexual M.P., Tom Driberg. He had been a society gossip columnist on the *Daily Express* and paradoxically had joined the British Communist Party in 1920. With contacts in the different worlds of politics, high society and the gay scene, he was an ideal informant for MI5 – although it was also rumoured he was also a KGB agent. Driberg was recruited in 1937 by the assistant director of Five responsible for counter-espionage, Maxwell Knight. He was in charge of planting 'moles' in fascist and communist organisations and other groups regarded by the government as a threat to national security. After 1933, Knight turned his attention to pro-German organisations operating in Britain.

After Tom Driberg was brought in, he introduced Crowley to the writer of adventure, historical and 'black magic' thrillers, Dennis Wheatley, whose wife worked as the transport administration officer for MI5. Wheatley was also personally recruited by Churchill to be part of a top secret unit in the Cabinet Office planning for total warfare (including the use of poison gas and biological weapons), the local defence of Britain if the Germans invaded, and organising a resistance movement if they succeeded. Crowley is supposed to have helped Wheatley with research for his occult novels and arranged introductions to other magicians. There is even a story that, while Wheatley denied ever attending any magical ceremony, he and Maxwell Knight might have become Crowley's students. Coincidentally, Dennis Wheatley was also a close friend of the occult writer Joan Grant, who wrote bestselling novels about reincarnation (such as *The Winged Pharaoh*), based on her own life in ancient Egypt. Grant practised Rosicrucian-type sex magic rites with her psychiatrist husband. She was also a member of the International Order of Co-Freemasonry and when this writer joined a Co-Masonic Egyptian-themed lodge in the 1970s, he was told that it was the one Joan Grant had been in many years before. Several of the members remembered her with fondness. As a child in 1914, she had sailed with her parents on the ill-fated *SS Lusitania*. Crowley was on the same voyage, and when in New York had visited Grant's family home because he knew her father (Spence, 2008 p226).

The incestuous connection between Maxwell Knight, Dennis Wheatley, Tom Driberg and Crowley is that all four men were interested in the occult. Knight was also obsessed with animals and kept grass snakes in the bath of his ground-floor Chelsea flat, an Amazonian parrot in the kitchen, and a Himalayan monkey in the garden. After the war, when he had retired from MI5, Knight started a successful second career. He recorded natural history programmes for BBC Radio's *Children's Hour* under the nickname of 'Uncle Mac'. Maxwell Knight was also bisexual and a friend of Lord Tredegar, who was mentioned earlier and also had a private menagerie.

When Knight's wife died in 1936 from a suspected accidental overdose of painkillers prescribed for her bad back, rumours circulated that she had committed suicide after participating in a magical ritual with Crowley. It was even suggested that she was murdered by her husband for her money, and the Great Beast had advised Knight how to do it using his knowledge of drugs (Spence, 2008, pp.226–7). Needless to say, there is not a shred of evidence to support either of these stories.

When war broke out, Crowley was eager to do his bit for king and country and continue his pre-war relationship with MI6. Both MI5 and the SIS approached and recruited occultists at the time because of their specialist knowledge and skills. On the 10th September 1939, seven days after the war started, and after filling in an application form, Crowley was invited to an interview at the Admiralty in Whitehall. This was with Commander C.J. Lang of the Naval Intelligence Department (NID). Only the two men know what happened at this secret meeting, but it has been claimed that when Crowley died in 1946, among his papers was found a note from the NID acknowledging his 'war efforts'.

Another possible clue to Crowley's wartime involvement with intelligence agencies surfaced in a report sent by the MI6 officer, British traitor and Soviet mole Kim Philby, to Moscow Control in 1942. Philby informed his Russian masters that MI6 were investigating a blackmailing racket linking Royal Air Force officers and members of British high society to drug smuggling, orgies (heterosexual and homosexual), and 'black magic rites'. It was believed that this racket was being run by operatives of the German secret service, based in their embassy in neutral Dublin. Coincidentally, Crowley's Berlin contact, Gerald Hamilton, was interned by the British in 1939 as a potential security risk. It was said that the government was worried about his 'suspicious communications' with the German Embassy in Dublin (Spence, 2008, p246).

According to Kim Philby, who supplied documentary evidence to the KGB that is strangely missing from SIS files, the 'notorious occultist Aleister Crowley' was involved in these nefarious activities (Tsarev and West, 1999, pp.316–8). Dr. Richard Spence believes that what the SIS stumbled upon was in fact a clandestine MI5 operation run by Maxwell Knight, possibly aided by Crowley. MI5 and MI6 have always been rivals, and often did not tell each other about ongoing operations. It may have been part of the sophisticated counter-espionage 'double-cross' system created by Five to 'turn' the Nazi spy network in Britain (ibid., p241). As both Crowley and, oddly, the Soviet ambassador are supposed to have been involved in organising the alleged sex orgies and Black Masses described by Philby, it is more likely that MI5 were behind it than the Germans. Intelligence services from all countries have always carried out 'false flag' operations and used the dark arts of blackmail and subversion to expose traitors and recruit foreign agents, politicians and dignitaries.

The assistant director of British Naval Intelligence during the Second World War was the eccentric, colourful and flamboyant Lt. Commander Ian Fleming R.N. He was, of course, to become world-famous in the 1950s as the creator of the fictional British spy, James Bond 007, who had a licence to kill. In fact, it is believed that Fleming based his character 'M' (the head of the Secret Service in the books) on his friend and colleague Maxwell Knight of MI5. It was also no mystery why Bond held the rank of a naval commander. Fleming also shared Knight's interest in the occult, especially astrology, divination and numerology, and he also knew Crowley. Hence, we have a clandestine social and work-related network of intelligence officers interested in occult and actual practitioners of the magical arts.

Commander Fleming was well-known for his innovative schemes, although some preferred to call them 'Ian's crazy ideas'. These included planning to snatch a German 'Enigma' code machine by staging a fake plane crash in the English Channel, scuttling barges made of cement in the Danube to block the river to Nazi shipping, forging millions of Reichmarks to bankrupt the German economy, and offering the French Navy the Isle of Wight as their sovereign territory for the duration of the war. He was a bit of a Boy's Own hero and created his own private commando unit called 30 Assault, known in the NID as 'the Red Indians', who were involved in daring raids on the coast of occupied Europe.

It may have been Fleming's interest in astrology that led his boss Admiral John Godfrey to recruit astrologers to cast the horoscopes of Hitler to see what he might be planning (or what the astrologers who worked for the Nazi were predicting and advising) and even those of our own Royal Navy admirals (recorded in a diary entry by MI5 chief, Guy Liddell, dated April 10th 1941, and quoted in Spence, 2008). One of the astrologers who it is known was recruited by SOE and the NID was a Hungarian-Jewish novelist, journalist and filmmaker called Louis de Wohl. He claimed that he had been given the honorary rank of a captain in the British Army by SOE, complete with a uniform. Although the Ministry of Defence denied this after the war, it was a known practice. The thriller writer Dennis Wheatley was given a temporary rank as a wing commander in the RAF Reserve to cover his secret wartime work (Howe, 1967, pp.204–5 and p215).

It was believed by the British government that Hitler and some high-ranking Nazis had an interest in such esoteric subjects as astrology, psychism, magic and the occult arts. In 1942, a secret psychiatric assessment was commissioned by British

Intelligence which concluded that Hitler was suffering from what it called 'religious delusions' and believed he was divine. The Fuehrer was also paranoid about the Jews and believed he was following a spiritual mission that in his twisted mind justified the policy of the Final Solution, resulting in the Holocaust. The report compared his ranting and near-hysterical speeches at the infamous nocturnal torchlit Nuremburg rallies to the work of a 'shaman' and he believed he was transmitting messages from 'the spirits' to his fanatical followers.

In 1943, the Office of Strategic Services (OSS), the wartime forerunner of the CIA, asked a well-known Harvard University psychologist to do a similar study. His report identified Hitler as someone suffering from a wide range of serious mental disorders. The doctor concluded, quite correctly, that if or when Germany faced defeat, its leader's messianic complex would mean he would take the ancient role of the 'dying god'. This meant he would sacrifice himself for his people and land by committing suicide (*The Times*, May 4th 2012).

Ian Fleming hatched an idea to exploit the known interest in the occult, divination and astrology by the German deputy fuehrer Rudolf Hess and his pre-war connections with Britain. He conceived a daring plan to lure the top Nazi to England by pretending to resurrect a pre-war Anglo-German friendship organisation called 'The Link'. Coincidentally, this had been formed by a retired director of the NID, Admiral Sir Barry Domvile, and included among its leading members an occultist called General J.F.C. Fuller, an open admirer of Hitler and a disciple of Crowley. Domvile was arrested and interned when the war began. This was because the government believed he was plotting a fascist coup, supported by appeasers in the British social and political establishment who wanted peace with Germany.

Ian Fleming's cunning plan was to plant disinformation that would be picked up by the German High Command.

The false intelligence would persuade them that despite its leading members being in prison, The Link was still operating underground. In fact, it still had secret supporters and friends in high places, including aristocrats and royalty. They were plotting to overthrow the 'warmonger' Churchill and his wartime coalition government and negotiate a truce and peace treaty with Nazi Germany. The British and Germans could then unite their armies to turn east and jointly fight the 'real enemy' – the communist Russians.

To achieve his aim, Fleming hired astrologers to produce fake charts and predictions to convince Hess to travel to Britain and meet up with representatives of The Link. The deputy fuehrer was fed data based on genuine astrological calculations which suggested that May 10th 1941 was an auspicious day for his trip. Coincidently, Hess also had a confirmatory dream in which he was having an audience at Buckingham Palace with King George, who he already falsely believed hated Churchill and wanted peace with his German cousins. It has been suggested that Crowley was employed by the NID to use magical or psychic techniques to plant the dream in Hess' mind while he slept (Spence, 2008, pp.247–8). When Hess carried out his disastrous 'peace mission' and landed by plane in Scotland, he was immediately arrested by the Home Guard and handed over to the Army. He had chosen a Scottish landing site near the ancestral home of the Duke of Hamilton, and he demanded to see the aristocrat. This was because he had been told that the duke was one of the secret members of the imaginary Link organisation and also a member of the Order of the Golden Dawn. Hess also said he wanted to be taken to London to see the king. Hess told his amazed interrogators that occultists had influenced or hypnotised Churchill to take a negative attitude towards Germany. He also said that the German High Command believed that key British political figures had been 'mesmerised by evil forces'. Allegedly, these same forces were trying to kill Hess because he was one of the few people that knew about their 'secret psychic powers' (*The Daily Telegraph*, 7th April, 2012). Naturally, the British authorities concluded that the deputy fuehrer was raving mad. In fact, one exasperated Army officer involved in his interrogation said that Hess should be taken out and shot like a rabid dog.

Commander Ian Fleming was keen that Crowley should be allowed to interview Hess in captivity. This seems to have been suggested to Fleming in a letter from Crowley, dated four days after the Nazi was captured. In it, the Great Beast says: 'If it is true that Herr Hess is much influenced by astrology and magick, my services might be useful to the [Naval Intelligence] department, in case he should not be willing to do as you wish' (Pearson, 1966). Although SIS asserted that Crowley never met Hess, it has been claimed that MI5 did arrange an interview between the two men at one of their interrogation centres. This was allegedly at Latchmore House on Ham Common in London, used by Five for questioning German prisoners of war and secret agents that they wanted to turn (Spence, 2008, p249).

The Nazi Party's reaction to Hess' 'peace mission' was to disown the deputy fuehrer and his actions. It was claimed that he was mentally deranged and had been falsely and disastrously influenced by astrologers and occultists. A report in *The Times* newspaper on May 14th 1941, however, claimed that Hess had secretly been offering astrological advice to Hitler. A few months before his ill-fated trip to Scotland, the deputy fuehrer had allegedly convinced himself from astrological calculations that, despite recent German victories, Hitler was doomed. Therefore, Hess saw it as his patriotic duty to try and make peace with the British government before Germany was defeated. Despite its unofficial interest, the Third Reich had always had an ambiguous official approach to occultism and secret societies. A few weeks after the failed mission, an operation called 'Aktion Hess' was launched by the Gestapo. This included banning performances or lectures on the occult, astrology, telepathy, clairvoyance and spiritualism, and many of their publicly known practitioners were arrested and ended up in concentration camps (Howe, 1967, pp.192–3).

Another occultist who was supposed to have been involved in or connected to the Hess affair was the late Cecil Hugh Williamson, the founder of the Museum of Witchcraft and Magic at Castletown on the Isle of Man, which is now located in Boscastle in North Cornwall. Williamson had been recruited into MI6 in 1938 by a family friend, Major Edward Maltby (who, coincidentally, was the brother-in-law of the famous occultist, Dion Fortune). He was described by a Six officer who met him at Warsaw Central railway station in 1939 as a typical English gentleman wearing his Old Etonian tie. As a supposed secret agent, his 'distinct haberdashery' made him stand out like a sore thumb among the Polish peasants coming off the train (Smith, 2010, p376).

The major was in charge of a section of SIS set up to deal with the unusual threat posed by esoteric and magical groups in Germany and occultists within the Nazi Party. Williamson agreed to work for Six as an undercover agent and, before the war, made several trips to Germany (posing as a folklorist) to collect information. Cecil told this writer that he believed the intelligence he collected on at least 2,000 Nazi Party members interested or involved in the occult and astrology helped Ian Fleming's NID operation to trap Rudolf Hess.

When the war started, Cecil Williamson was seconded to a specialist unit of the Special Executive Operation (SOE), based at Woburn Abbey in Bedfordshire. Churchill had ordered the formation of the SOE to work with resistance groups in Nazi-occupied Europe and organise and take part in subversion, sabotage and assassinations. Williamson worked initially with Edward Maltby, who was then a Lieutenant Colonel and assistant director of the communications section of MI6 – the Radio Security Service that Lord Tredegar worked for in London.

Williamson's immediate boss was an ex-*Daily Express* journalist, Sefton Delmer, who ran the Psychological Warfare Executive (PWE) involved in 'black' propaganda. Delmer had also been involved with Ian Fleming in the Hess operation. Dr. Spence refers to a long-destroyed intelligence file on '*The Use of Astrology in Propaganda*' and he suggests that Delmer was in charge of the astrological aspects of the affair (Spence, 2008, p251). Another possibility is that it was Sir Charles Hambro, the deputy director of SOE, who had commissioned Louis de Wohl to furnish it with material that could be used for 'black' propaganda. He also sent the Hungarian astrologer to America on a lecture tour predicting the downfall of Nazi Germany based on astrological predictions (Howe, 1967, pp.210–3).

One of the tasks of the PWE was to run 'black' propaganda radio stations, feeding false information to the German High Command and morale-sapping news to German U-boats patrolling the Atlantic. Williamson was given the job of controlling several static and mobile radio stations located across Southern England, including the New Forest area. These had been secretly supplied by the American government, and Williamson supervised the mobile ones operated from the back of army trucks. These were camouflaged and kept moving around so that they were not a tempting target for the Luftwaffe. These radio units broadcast an entertaining mixture of American and British jazz and dance band music, interspersed with 'news' describing the kinky sex activities and financial corruption of the Nazi hierarchy back home, and fake astrological predictions and prophecies by the medieval French seer Nostradamus about a German defeat in the war (possibly supplied to SOE by Louis de Wohl).

One of Cecil Williamson's most controversial claims relating to his wartime work was his involvement in an anti-Hitler propaganda exercise, organised jointly by the SIS and MI5, called Operation Mistletoe, which may or may not have included Crowley's participation. This was supposed to have taken place in

Ashdown Forest in Sussex and featured a fake magical ritual. Its aim was to convince those in the German High Command who believed in the occult that ceremonial magicians and witches in England were working against them. Allegedly, Canadian troops were recruited to take part in the 'ritual' – acting as 'wizards' and wearing improvised 'robes' made from sacking, decorated with symbols from the Key of Solomon. Doubt has been cast on the truth of Williamson's account, and partly because Canadian and not British troops were involved. However, a radio transmitter with a tall tower (code-named 'Aspidistra') was provided by the US military and set up in Ashdown Forest. This was as part of the work Williamson was responsible for, and a Canadian engineer battalion based locally was brought in to erect it.

According to an obituary of Cecil Williamson, published in the *Daily Telegraph* newspaper when he died in 1999, he also carried out undercover operations with the SOE in occupied France. This may still have been part of his work with the Radio Security Service, as one of its tasks was to make and supply small radio transmitters to SOE agents working with the French Resistance. Towards the end of the war, Williamson and the RSS were part of Operation Fortitude. This was a complex and sophisticated plan to mislead the Germans that the expected Allied invasion of Europe would take place on the French coast at Pas de Calais, rather than the real site of the D-Day landings in Normandy. Williamson's job was to broadcast false messages about army manoeuvres in Essex, preparing for the invasion – rather than the real ones on the south coast of England (Heselton, 2012, Vol.2, pp.412-3).

As well as those occultists working in military intelligence, others were also doing magic against the Nazis – especially in the early days of the war when a German invasion was expected any day and Britain was unprepared. One famous example is the ritual at Lammas in 1940 (or possibly a series of rituals on the full moons from May Eve to Lammas), carried out by the New Forest

Coven and vividly described by Gerald Gardner. He also claimed that the local hereditary witches in the coven had told him that their ancestors did similar magical rituals to stop the Spanish Armada and Napoleon's proposed invasion of England (Heselton, 2012, Vol.1, pp.240–52). Incidentally, Cecil Williamson had family connections to the New Forest, and one of the RSS transmitters was based there in the war. He told this writer that, at that period, he had come across Gardner's initiator, 'Dafo' (Edith Woodford-Grimes), and also met other witches in the area who had nothing to do with the New Forest Coven.

The anti-Nazi activities of Dion Fortune and her Fraternity of the Inner Light during the war have been given the title 'The Magical Battle of Britain' (see Knight, 1993). According to a letter from Geraldine Beskin, owner of the Atlantis occult bookshop in Museum Street, London, published in the paranormal magazine *Fortean Times* #288 (May, 2012), in her opinion, Dion Fortune's rituals to protect Britain from the Nazis were ironic. This was because her family, the Firth's, based in Sheffield, were the 'world's largest producers of arms and armaments'. Beskin said that in the nineteenth-century, steel from the Firth foundry was used to manufacture all the guns supplied to the British government. It may well be ironic, but perhaps Dion Fortune's magical rituals were just an extension on another level of the valuable services her family had provided for the British Empire in the past?

As mentioned earlier, Dion Fortune had a link (by marriage) with Cecil Williamson's MI6 recruiter, Major Edward Maltby. Both he and another MI6 officer, Anthony Daws, belonged to a magical lodge led by Christine Hartley (one of Fortune's students and, at one time, her heir apparent until they fell out) and Hartley's magical partner, Charles Richard Foster 'Kim' Seymour. Interestingly, and perhaps highly coincidentally, Colonel Seymour – an Irishman who had served in the Indian Army, taken part in 'covert actions' in Iraq during the First World

War and worked as a Russian translator – was employed by the War Office to intercept and study enemy messages. Using his specialist knowledge, his job description included investigating links between British and German occult groups. Later, Seymour joined the SIS, and during the war he became the head of the Dutch section of the SOE (Jeffrey, 2010, p544).

There were also attempts to curse Hitler and, again, Crowley was involved. In 1941, he wrote *Thumbs-Up: A Pentagram – A Panticle to Win the War*, which was privately published from his then-home at 10 Hanover Square in a posh district of London's West End, and by the American branch of the OTO at the 'Abbey of Thelema' in California. It includes patriotic poems by Crowley: *England, Stand Fast!* and *Hymn for the American People*, and a curse against Adolf Shicklegruber – Hitler's real Austrian name.

Also in 1941, the American writer, globetrotting adventurer and occultist William B. Seabrook was contacted by a 'coven' of amateur witches in Washington asking for instruction on how to do 'doll magic' against Hitler. Their representative, Richard W. Tupper, told Seabrook that 'it would help pass the evenings' and also perhaps encourage thousands of people to hex Herr Hitler. Seabrook was delighted with the idea, as he had plenty of experience with witch poppets and wax images in pre-war France, London and New York. He also said, interestingly: 'After all, it was Hitler who invented psychic warfare.' Seabrook even provided Mr Tupper and his Washington witches with a suitable hexing charm that they could use when sticking pins in an effigy of the German leader:

> *Islan, come and help us,*
> *We are driving pins and needles,*
> *Into Adolf Hitler's heart,*
> *We are driving pins and needles,*
> *Driving pins and needles,*
> *Cat will claw his heart,*
> *Dog will bite it in the night.*

Islan, Seabrook helpfully explained for those who have never heard of him before, was a Pagan god worshipped in Central Europe in the Middle Ages.

The story appeared in the March 1941 issue of the popular magazine, *Readers Digest*, which is still published and can often be found in doctors' surgeries and dentists' waiting rooms. On 13th May, coinciding with the announcement on American radio of the capture of Rudolf Hess by the British three days earlier, a *Digest* reader called Fred W. Schultz wrote to the magazine, suggesting that 'hexing Hitler' should be on a mass-production scale. He referred to a 'negress' named Katherine Durham who was an anthropologist and had studied voodoo in Haiti and had noted that the American movie industry was making educational and propaganda films for the US military.

Schultz says in his letter that William Seabrook and Katherine Durham could combine their knowledge of 'jungle magic' (sic) to write more incantations and suggest suitable material for making a Hitler doll. He added that the Walt Disney Corporation or the International Ladies Garment Workers Union could design, produce and sell such a doll, accompanied with hexing instructions. Disney could also release a short film or cartoon of a 'hexing Hitler' session so that people could copy it. Schultz copied his letter to Durham and the Walt Disney studios in Hollywood. Their reaction is unknown, but no Hitler doll ever came onto the market.

However, during the Second World War, small figurines of Hitler depicting him bending over with his trousers down were marketed and proved successful. His bare backside was a pincushion, and no doubt could be used like a wax image for cursing. The pincushions were copied from a similar popular image of 'Kaiser Bill' (the German Emperor Wilhelm) sold in the First World War. Examples of both figures are on display in the witchcraft museum at Boscastle.

It is also possible that, behind the scenes, British Intelligence was also involved in hands-on occult operations that were more real and serious than Operation Mistletoe. Again, as in the Ashdown Forest event, unsubstantiated rumours linked Aleister Crowley with one incident. In April of 1943, four boys searching for birds' nests in Hagley Wood in Warwickshire found the skeletal remains in an old hollowed-out elm tree. The police were called, and it was established that the bones were the remains of a woman aged about 30. Scraps of rotted clothing, a pair of shoes and a cheap wedding ring were also found. At first, it seemed as if the skeleton was complete – but upon further investigation, it was found that the right hand was missing. It was later found some yards away from the tree. From forensic evidence and a witness who came forward saying he had heard screams in the wood at the time, it was believed that the remains had been placed in the tree about two years prior.

Various theories were put forward about the incident. Naturally, Dr. Margaret Alice Murray came forward to claim it was a sign of the revival of ancient tree worship and was a human sacrifice to some arboreal god or spirit. Obviously, the media picked up on this sensational theory, and suddenly the skeleton in the tree was a witch or the victim of witchcraft. As is to be expected, the detectives investigating the case were less than convinced by the theory. The concept of tree sacrifice incidentally features in Robin Hardy's new movie, *The Wicker Tree*, which is a follow-up to the classic 1970s horror film, *The Wicker Man*. About eight months after the grisly find, graffiti began appearing on walls and monuments in Birmingham saying: 'Who put Bella down in the wych-elm?' and 'Hagley Wood Bella'. Sometimes, her name was spelt 'Luebella'. Normally, no notice would have been taken of such public scribblings, except that Bella was an unusual and foreign-sounding name.

Writer Donald McCormick came across the 'Bella-in-a-tree' case when investigating the gory ritualistic murder in 1945 of an elderly farm labourer called Charles Walton in the village of Lower Quinton, also in Warwickshire. Allegedly, he was another victim of human sacrifice (according to Dr. Murray), despite his age! There were also rumours that Crowley and some of his disciples from Cornwall and the Midlands were involved in the killing. In fact, Walton was known locally as a 'cunning man' and may have been killed because somebody feared his powers. More prosaically, it was suggested that he was the victim of a dispute with a local farmer over money he was owed. McCormack, however, suggested that both murders were connected with a revival of witchcraft before the war in the West Midlands and Cotswolds. Allegedly, a 'Hungarian astrologer' working for British Intelligence was involved in setting up several new covens in the area. As McCormick had worked for the SIS and later wrote a history of the British Secret Service under the nom de plume 'Richard Deacon', he may have had some inside knowledge to support this claim.

McCormick says that the pre-war traditional witch covens established in the Cotswolds were authentic (which suggests that genuine people were involved) but were part of an intelligence operation to catch Nazi spies. He claimed that agents of the Third Reich had been parachuted into the Midlands from occupied Holland in 1941, and MI5 had uncovered the plot. McCormick had met an ex-Nazi who had spent some time in the Midlands during the war and knew a German agent with a Dutch girlfriend called Clarabella Dronkers. Coincidentally, in 1942, a Dutchman called Johannes Marinus Dronkers was executed by the British for spying.

Allegedly, McCormick then discovered from an informant in Holland who knew Clarabella that she had been a member of the Dutch Resistance and therefore would have probably had SOE contacts. However, her Resistance colleagues suspected that Clarabella was a double agent working for the Germans. She was also interested in astrology and the occult and owned a so-called 'witch's garter' made of green snakeskin. It is true that two German parachutists were supposed to have landed and then vanished in the Hagley Wood area in 1941.

In 1953, a local newspaper reporter in Wolverhampton was contacted by somebody called 'Anna'. She claimed that the woman (nicknamed 'Bella') had been murdered because she knew too much about a pro-Nazi spy ring, whose members included an RAF officer who was a traitor. According to the informant, who claimed to have known 'Bella', she had entered England illegally from Holland and got mixed up in espionage. Like the Walton murder, the case was never solved and, mysteriously and very suspiciously, both the 'Bella' skeleton and her clothing subsequently went 'missing' (Newman, 2009, p85, and McCormick, 1968). So it would seem that there is a lot of evidence of occult activities during the Second World War involving secret agents, magicians and the Nazis. The links between occultists and the intelligence community were not confined to wartime. Behind the Profumo Affair in 1963, which nearly led to the fall of the Tory government, there was a strong occult element that was covered up. The scandal featured politicians, high society orgies, call girls, MI5 and Russian spies. At least two of the leading figures in the affair were practitioners of what the sensationalist press would call 'black magic'. In recent times, the CIA and the KGB have both employed clairvoyants, conducted scientific research into the use of psychic powers for espionage and warfare, and also carried out mind-control experiments. If the rumours and leaks are true, as Cecil Williamson said about old-style witchcraft, it still goes on today.

Acknowledgements to Levannah Morgan and Graham King for the information on 'hexing Hitler', and Paul Busby for the intelligence on Lord Tredegar and his occult activities.

BIBLIOGRAPHY AND REFERENCES:

Andrew, Christopher (2009) *The Defence of the Realm: The Authorized History of MI5*. Allen Lane.

Jeffrey, Keith (2009) *MI6: The History of the Secret Intelligence Service 1909–1949*. Bloomsbury.

Heselton, Philip (2012) *Witchfinder: A Life of Gerald Gardner. Vols. 1 and 2*. Thoth Publications.

Howe, Ellic (1967) *Urania's Children: The Strange World of the Astrologers*. William Kimber.

Knight, Gareth and Fortune, Dion (1993) *The Magical Battle of Britain*. Golden Gate Press.

McCormick, Donald (1968) *Murder by Witchcraft*. Arrow.

McGinty, Stephen (2011) *Camp Z: The Secret Life of Rudolf Hess*. Quercus.

Newman, Paul (2009) *Under the Shadow of Meon Hill: The Lower Quinton & Hagley Wood Murders*. Abraxas Publications.

Pearson, John (1966) *The Life of Ian Fleming*. Companion Books.

Picknett, Lynn; Prince, Clive; and Prior, Stephen; with Brydon, Robert (2011) *Double Standards: The Rudolf Hess Cover-Up*. Little Brown & Company.

Rankin, Nicolas (2011) *Ian Fleming's Commandos: The Story of 30 Assault Unit*. Faber.

Smith, Michael (2010) *Six: A History of Britain's Secret Intelligence Service; Part One – Murder and Mayhem 1909-1939*. Dialogue.

Spence, Dr. Richard (2008) *Secret Agent 666: Aleister Crowley, British Intelligence and the Occult*. USA: Feral House.

Tsarev, Oleg; and West, Nigel (1999) *The Crown Jewels: The British Secrets at the Heart of the KGB Archives*. New Haven/Yale University Press.

Published by kind permission of the estate of Micheal Howard.

The Old Ones in the Old Book

PHILIP WEST

Most Western people are familiar with the main plot of the Bible's Old Testament: the only true God (a male deity called Yahweh) reveals himself to Abraham, rescues his people from slavery in Egypt under Moses, gives them the Ten Commandments in the Sinai Desert, and then gives them the land of Israel to live in. He insists that they worship him alone, rejecting utterly the Pagan gods of the surrounding peoples.

At first sight, such a book seems to have little to offer Pagans. It is dominated by an exclusive male deity and it has an emphasis on history – to the neglect of nature – but scratch the surface of its texts, and things are very different. Because although the 'official line' of the Old Testament is monotheistic as above, this monotheism is really only a gloss applied to it by late editors. The more ancient texts themselves bear witness to a religion practised in Israel before 600 BCE which was very different. Far from being a stern monotheism, it was a colourful polytheistic Paganism.

ISRAEL AND CANAAN

According to the Old Testament's official editorial line, the Israelites' occupation of their promised land (then called Canaan, later called Israel) was one of violent conquest and genocide. Their leader Joshua "defeated the whole land, the hill country and the Negeb and the lowland and the slopes, and all their kings; he left none remaining, but utterly destroyed all that breathed, as

Yahweh the God of Israel commanded[1]." This suggests that the Israelites had no positive contact at all with the Canaanites they displaced and, in particular, that the Asherah Israelite religion was totally different from the religion of the Canaanites.

The ancient texts themselves tell a different story, however. They tell of a gradual and largely peaceful settlement, rather than united conquest[2], and of an Israelite religion which emerged out of the Canaanite religion, retaining many of its features. Fortunately, we now have good independent knowledge of that ancient Canaanite religion from finds at Ugarit in Syria[3], and the parallels between it and the religion of the Old Testament are striking.

EL AND BAAL

The parallels begin with the very word 'God': *elohim* in Hebrew, the language of the Old Testament. The word translated as 'God' (*elohim*) in our Bibles is a plural ('gods'). This immediately suggests a polytheistic Israelite past where the people worshipped a pantheon of gods, rather than a single deity. Moreover, its singular form (*el*) is the name of the chief high god of the Canaanite pantheon, 'El', as known from Ugarit[4]. So, when the Old Testament talks of "God", it does so using the name of a Canaanite god.

Even more significantly, the characteristics of Canaanite El underlie many of the features of 'God' as shown in the Bible as a whole. His titles include "Father of Humankind", "Creator of the Earth", "King", and "the Friendly One" – none of which applied to the rather dangerous, sinister and passionate Yahweh who

---

[1] Joshua 10.40 (the Book of Joshua, chapter 10, verse 40).
[2] Judges 1.
[3] See John Gray: *The Canaanites* (Thames & Hudson 1964) and J.C.L. Gibson: *Canaanite Myths and Legends* (T&T Clark, 2004).
[4] Ancient Hebrew was much more like a dialect of Canaanite than a separate language; so many words are common between the two cultures.

was revealed to Moses in the desert. Indeed, the more attractive attributes of wisdom, patience, mercy, and compassion for the weak of the later biblical God can be traced back to this Pagan Canaanite source – not to anything distinctly Israelite at all.

Something similar applies to a second Canaanite god, Baal. At Ugarit, he was the God of Storms, Rain and Fertility, with titles such as "Mighty One", "Ruler", "Rider on the Clouds", and "Prince of the Earth". Now, 'Baal' was in fact another title for the god, meaning 'Lord' (his proper name was Hadad) – and as this was a title suitable for virtually any powerful male deity, many Yahweh-worshippers readily equated Baal with Yahweh and used the same title for Yahweh as well. So, when the Old Testament and modern evangelical Christians talk about God (or Christ) as 'The Lord', they are again using a title with its deepest roots in a Pagan Canaanite deity.

As with El, many of Canaanite Baal's features were adopted into the Israelite conception of God, changing some of his characteristics. And also adopted were several hymns addressed to them both. Old Testament scholars believe that Bible Psalms 19, 29 and 68 were originally Canaanite hymns addressed to these pagan deities.

ASHERAH

A third Canaanite god known from Ugarit was Asherah, the female consort of El and mother of the gods. She was the most approachable face of the pantheon, and could intercede effectively with the more remote El on behalf of others. Compare here the role of the Blessed Virgin Mary in Roman Catholic Christianity, who may have her roots here.

It is quite clear that the majority of Israelites worshipped Asherah alongside Yahweh, at least until the exile in 587 BCE, despite the vitriol poured on this practice by the later monotheistic editors. The 'high places' (sanctuaries) regularly featured wooden pillars which represented her[5], as did the temple itself[6]. Her priests were numerous in the capital and were sponsored by the Israelite royal family[7], and the editors blamed the eventual destruction of the Northern Kingdom of Israel on its people, having "set up for themselves pillars and Asherim (a plural of Asherah) on every high hill and under every green tree[8]."

SACRIFICE

The crucial finds at Ugarit also provide valuable comparative material about ancient Israelite worship. This worship, far from being unique (as the late editors believed), was, in fact, essentially Canaanite.

Israelite worship centred upon sacrifice, and all three forms of sacrifice found in the Old Testament are identical to ancient Canaanite practices. The most important was 'sacrifice proper' – in which the blood of a sacrificial animal was poured over the altar and its fat and entrails were burned to provide a pleasing smoke for the deity. The meat was then cooked and shared by priest and worshippers in a communion meal at the god's table. So here, in ancient Canaanite religion, is the deepest root of the present-day Christian Holy Communion or Mass.

In addition, the locations for this worship (the 'high places'), the forms of the sacrificial priesthood, and the annual festivals were all taken over from the Canaanites pretty much lock, stock and barrel.

---

5 See Judges 6.25-32, 1 Kings 15.13, and many other places.
6 2 Kings 23.6.
7 1 Kings 18.19.
8 2 Kings 17.10.

FESTIVALS

Ancient Israel kept several agricultural festivals which, in typical pagan fashion, attuned her with the cycle of the seasons. The most important were the Feast of Unleavened Bread at the beginning of the barley harvest, the Feast of Weeks at the wheat harvest, and the Feast of Ingathering – the autumn harvest festival. The late editors trace the origins of these to institutions by Moses in the Sinai Desert, but this is clearly not the case – they were simply local agricultural methods adopted by the incoming pastoralist Israelites.

All of these festivals involved a great deal of Canaanite fertility religion and nothing whatever of the worship of Yahweh. For example, for the last one, the whole community would take a week's holiday, camping out in the orchards and vineyards, and sleeping in huts made of branches. The new wine flowed freely, and mating between the young men and women was facilitated.

The later monotheistic editors reinterpreted these festivals in terms of sacred history and the worship of Yahweh (compare the Christian reinterpretations of Christmas and Easter). Most notably, the Feast of Unleavened Bread (at which, to mark a new beginning, bread from the new grain was eaten without the addition of any old dough containing yeast) was transformed into the Feast of Passover. This became a memorial of the escape of the people from Egypt after the angel of death had 'passed over' the Israelite houses and entered only the Egyptian houses to kill their first-born[9] – but its Canaanite agricultural origins account for the otherwise inexplicable detail in the story that the people were ordered to eat unleavened bread before their escape[10].

---

9 Exodus 12.21-32.
10 Exodus 12.14-20.

DAVID AND JERUSALEM

When, in about 1000 BCE, King David captured the Canaanite city of Jerusalem and made it his capital city, yet another set of Canaanite ideas and practices entered Israelite religion. In fact, rather than imposing a distinctively Israelite religion on the city, he slotted himself into the city's political and religious system as its next Canaanite ruler.

This is clear in the case of the priesthood. The Canaanite ('Zadokite') priesthood from Jerusalem was henceforth placed in charge of the Israelite sacrificial system, displacing the Israelite priesthood from their leadership roles (a poor attempt by the later editors to disguise this by tracing the lineage of the new priesthood back to Moses in the desert is pretty transparent) – but even more important was the elevation of the figure of the king to semi-divine status, following the pattern of 'sacral kingship' found among the Canaanites.

Although the king was never actually regarded as a god in ancient Israel, he was from now on believed to be adopted by Yahweh as His son at his coronation. This gave the king a position far transcending that of any other human being, endowed with superabundant life and with a seat at Yahweh's right hand, sharing his sovereignty. The blessings of Yahweh flowed through him to his people and the land, making him the main conduit between heaven and earth. And in the other direction, he became the high priest of the cult – uniquely able to offer effective sacrifices to Yahweh on behalf of his people.

This relationship is colourfully displayed in the 'royal psalms' of the Old Testament, used at the coronation of the king. For example:

> "Yet I have set my king upon my holy hill of Zion ... Thou art my Son; this day have I begotten thee. Ask of me, and I [conclusion] 'will make the nations your heritage and the ends of the earth your property[11].'"

---
11 Psalm 2.6-8.

Later on, the earliest Christians took these psalmic references to refer to Christ, and borrowed for him the title 'Son of God' – originally applied to the Canaanite kings. In doing so, they unwittingly incorporated a Pagan element into their new religion – one completely unconnected with the original faith of Yahweh.

SOLOMON AND THE TEMPLE

To the late editors of the Old Testament, the Jerusalem Temple built by David's son Solomon in the mid-tenth century BCE was the centre of the religion of Yahweh – but what these editors did not appreciate was that the temple was a thoroughly Pagan construction.

A comparison of it, as described in the Old Testament, with several contemporary temples in Syria and Palestine shows that it was indistinguishable from other sanctuaries of the same period. Like a standard Canaanite temple, it has three rooms in a line. It had extensive decorations of pomegranates[12] – a standard fertility symbol echoing the Baal myths. It contained a bronze sea supported by twelve bronze oxen[13] symbolizing the mother goddess from whose body the universe was created in ancient Near Eastern myth – and the construction work was done by the craftsmen of Hiram, King of Tyre, who built it along familiar lines[14].

In addition, the sacrificial worship going on inside the Author Temple was Canaanite in form, as was all Israelite worship of the time – and the following list of things removed from it during the reforms of Josiah in the seventh century BCE shows that its worship was far from directed solely towards Yahweh:

---

12 1 Kings 7.42.
13 1 Kings 7.23-26.
14 1 Kings 5-7.

- Vessels made for Baal, Asherah and "all the host of heaven" (that is, a variety of other heavenly beings or gods).
- An Asherah (a wooden pillar representing the goddess).
- Male cult prostitutes and their homes (which implies the practice in the temple of a Canaanite fertility cult – possibly the female cult prostitutes were left in place?).
- Women who wove hangings for Asherah.
- Statues of horses, plus chariots, dedicated to the sun (the sun was a common deity in the ancient Near East).
- Alters to a variety of other unnamed deities[15].

It seems that the temple was a general sanctuary for the worship of a variety of gods, albeit possibly with Yahweh as the chief, rather than just a home for Yahweh himself, as the late editors believed.

CONCLUSION

So, gentle reader, perhaps the time has come to dust off your neglected copy of the Old Testament and dip into it? Within its confines are to be found many conducive things, of which this article offers only a selection. Traces of the Old Ones are to be found there, even within the pages of the Old Book.

AUTHOR

Philip West has degrees in theology from London and Cambridge universities and is a member of The Pagan Federation. His first book, *The Old Ones in the Old Book: Pagan Roots of the Hebrew Old Testament*, is published by Moon Books (2012).

See www.philip-west.com/books.html for details, and www.philip-west.com/order.html for ordering.

---

15 2 Kings 23.4-12.

The Web of Wyrd and the Runes

NIGEL PENNICK

"On the horn's face were there
All the kinds of letters
Cut right and reddened.
How should I read them rightly?"
—from the ancient *First Lay of Guðrún*.

Northern Tradition philosophy describes existence as a universal fabric that interconnects everything there ever was, is, or will be. It is the Web of Wyrd; people, things and events are seen traditionally as being all interwoven in the web. Wyrd is an Old English word which comes from *weorðan*, meaning 'to become', 'to come into being' or 'to come to pass'. A connected meaning is 'to turn', and, in the context of Wyrd, this means how events have turned out. The word Wyrd refers to an individual's 'lot in life', his or her position in the world, with all its limitations and possibilities – something often referred to as one's destiny or fate. But the Northern Tradition does not have the concept of fate as something which predestines us to undergo unavoidable events which somehow have been written in advance. The contemporary usage of the words 'fate' and 'destiny' contains ideas of unavoidable predestiny, but our Wyrd does not necessarily doom us to a particular fate – but we are where we are. An Anglo-Saxon saying meaning 'that is my lot in life' is *me thet wyrd gewaef* – 'Wyrd wove me that'.

The Web of Wyrd is viewed like a weaving – constantly being added to and constantly disintegrating. In the European Tradition, the processes ruling destiny are personified as three sisters. In ancient Greece, they were the Moirai; in Roman Paganism, the Three Fates; in the Northern Tradition, they are the Norns or Weird Sisters. Whatever they are called in the different traditions, they are personified as three women involved in weaving fabric. The first woman spins the thread; the second weaves it into a fabric; and the third tears it apart.

The first signifies the beginning, which is the past; the second, the formative, creative process of existence, which is the present; and the third, destruction, which is the future. In the Northern Tradition, their names are Urd, 'That Which Was'; Verdandi, 'That Which Is'; and Skuld, 'That Which Is To Become'. The warp of the woven fabric of the Web of Wyrd is seen as time and events, whilst the weft is composed of individual human acts. As the process of weaving the web continues, the pattern of interactions of the threads, which are lives and events, irreversibly come together to exist for a while before being torn apart.

The Web of Wyrd is a symbolic description of the reality in which we live. In Europe, traditional indigenous spirituality does not diminish the reality of physical matter as an illusion. Neither is it considered to be 'fallen' – tainted with evil and thus less real than the spirit. Nor does it view matter materialistically as lifeless, dead stuff, devoid of creative potential. Nature is paramount – for without Nature, we have no being. Wyrd is the operating principle of Nature. Wyrd embodies the fundamental structures and processes that manifest themselves continually as recognisable elements of the physical world. These principles can reveal themselves spontaneously, or may be identified by human intelligence. Traditional spirituality recognises them as divine principles that operate throughout the cosmos, from the smallest particle through into everything that exists and has existed. In this sense, the visible world is an emanation of the invisible.

The true principles of Wyrd are often viewed as the signature of divinity.

Like a piece of fabric already woven, Wyrd is something that cannot be altered or undone – either we can be passive and allow the vagaries of life to defeat us; or we can deal creatively with the situation in which we find ourselves. There is an old traditional saying from north-east England: "Let us dree our wyrd" – which tells us that, once we stop complaining and accept our Wyrd, we can turn its disadvantages into our advantages. We are within our given circumstances, living in our own time, and must endure their accompanying difficulties – but how we endure them and how we deal with our circumstances is up to us. Wyrd works in accordance with nature – all things that come to individuals are neither rewards nor punishments sent by the gods, but rather they are the inevitable consequences of our own and other people's actions – whatever happens to us spiritually is the result of how we react to the conditions in which we find ourselves, for we have free will and choice of how to act within our circumstances. Even the gods are not outside Wyrd, but are subject to it – like we are. This is clear from original texts from both Northern Paganism and traditional Anglo-Saxon Christianity. As an Old English gnomic verse in one of the Cottonian manuscripts tells us: "The glories of Christ are great: Wyrd is strongest of all."

Speaking of the Norns, the ancient Icelandic poem, *Völuspá* (*The Sybil's Vision*), recounts that, "Staves did cut, laws did they make, lives did they choose: for the children of men they marked their fates." The Norns name is interpreted as *those who speak* – related to the Middle English verb *nurnen*, which means 'to say'. The Norns' utterances or decrees are expressed in the form of runic writing – the 'staves'. Staves can mean both runic characters and the wooden staves upon which they are cut – the rune staves being cut upon a rune-staff. The runes are fundamental to understanding something of the weavings of the Web of Wyrd and our place within it. When we use the runes, we can penetrate the surface of outward appearances – and enter the realm of consciousness that perceives the basic unity of life that is the Web of Wyrd. Even in the everyday prosaic use of characters to represent sounds and numbers, we penetrate some of the mysteries which lie at the foundations of existence. At the basic level, the individual runes are various patterns that occur within the Web of Wyrd and serve us to grasp the nature of these patterns.

The runes have a special place in the Northern Tradition. The alphabetic glyphs or signs that we call runes are what appear in the mind when the word *rune* is heard. But a rune is much more than just a letter in an alphabet; as well as possessing symbolic meaning either as an alphabet letter, an ideogram or a symbol, it can also mean a song, a poem, an incantation or an invocation. The word *rune* itself means 'a mystery' – the Old English word *run* and the Middle Welsh word *rhin*. Within the simple letter, composed of a few lines, lies a great deal more than its surface appearance. At its basic level, a rune denotes a mystery that is something secret and Otherworldly, something which is more than just an unknown meaning for a person who is illiterate or uninterested. Each rune stave is a unit of embedded lore, a storehouse of knowledge and meaning within human consciousness. According to the Northern Tradition worldview, the interconnections of the nerve pathways in the brain are an obvious aspect of the Web of Wyrd. As a symbol, a rune denotes a formless and eternal reality that is rooted in the world as we experience it.

If not earlier, during the late Bronze Age and the transition to the Iron Age (circa 1300–800 BCE), centuries before they became a means of communicating any specific message between people, many individual runestaves originated as pictographic symbols, scratched and cut onto rock surfaces, and probably also on perishable materials like wood, leather and fabric, now destroyed. About 2,000 years ago, some of these symbols were identified with letters from the Etruscan alphabet from Southern Europe, and a new phonetic futhark, named after the orders of the letters (which is not the same as the Greek, Roman and Etruscan alphabets) came into being, perhaps in Central Europe in what is now Austria. It was an act of creative genius to link ancient meanings of pictograms with sounds and meanings of the alphabet, and it is found in the ancient Norse scripture, *The Edda*, where it was through Odin (master of magic, poetry and inspiration) that this synthesis – or rather, realisation – took place. Odin is known as Woden in the English tradition, a name whose element *wod* denotes divine ecstasy. In the song of *Hávamál* (*Utterances of the High One*), stanzas 138 and 139 read:

> "I know that I hung on that windswept tree,
> Through nine days and nine nights,
> I was pierced with a spear,
> And given to Odin,
> Myself to myself,
> On that tree, which no man knows,
> From which roots it rises.
> Nor drinking horn.
> I took up the runes,
> Screaming I took them,
> Then I fell back from that place."

As *Hávamál*, which is an ethical spiritual text containing the wise sayings of Odin, exhorts us in the next verses: "Hidden runes you shall seek, and interpreted signs; many signs of might and main by the great Singer painted, by the High Powers fashioned, engraved by the Utterer of the gods."

This account of an experience of altered consciousness, brought on through a terrifying and life-changing trauma, is recognisable to any who have undergone such an ordeal, willingly or by accident. The psychic trauma of being close to death dismembers the old persona and, if the individual survives, he or she is reconstructed in a subtly different manner, whose worldview is irrevocably altered. Such experiences are sometimes perceived by people who undergo them as breaking through from the realm of everyday awareness into eldritch realms of being that are imperceptible in normal states of consciousness. Shamans, willingly or not, undergo traumatic experiences through which they gain access to other states of consciousness and communication with the denizens of the Otherworld.

In the story of Odin, the runes were gained by shamanic self-sacrifice, and once obtained from the Otherworld, they were available ever after for use by humans. There are two main routes of rune use, one incoming and the other outgoing. The incoming use of the runes is to employ them as an oracle in runic divination, while the outgoing use is to project their power in rune magic. Both divination and magic operate according to the state of the Web of Wyrd. Runic divination gives a reading of the parts of Wyrd that the diviner wishes to examine, telling her or him what is and what is not possible at the present time. Glimpses of certain inexpressible aspects of the Web of Wyrd that we need to know about may be gained by using the runes in divination. Rune magic uses the operative principles inherent in Wyrd to produce results willed by the rune magician. There are ancient texts which record runic spells that address every possibility of human interaction with the world and with other people. There are runic binding spells, love spells, spells for gain, gambling magic, magic for combat and binding; they provide protection against harm, and the means to distinguish beneficial divinities from harmful sprites. These ancient texts are the basis for all rune magic, but one needs the subtle understanding of the runes in order to use them effectively. When we work with the runes, we are working with archetype principles we can understand. Through rune work, we use our skills to the best of our abilities to bring the external forms of matter and events into harmony with them. By studying the runes, we can perceive these simple truths emanating from Wyrd and work with them in a positive way. To us at least, the various runes are symbolic presentations of the infinite – unveiling to us hitherto-unrealised parts of our existence. At such places and moments, the distinction between the self and the external other loses its significance. We are in harmony with Wyrd.

The Magic of the Thracians is still Alive …

GEORGI MISHEV

In the depths of the Strandzha Mountains, near the small village of Zabernovo, there in the European Southeast, in a country now known as Bulgaria, part of the vast region called by the ancient Greeks Thracia, amidst the oaks snuggling down, lays a discreet building, a chapel. At first sight, there is nothing unusual in this scene; it is actually something typical for most of the rural areas of the Balkan Peninsula. But is this really a usual scene, or does this structure keep inside a secret, a token of the spirit of antiquity? The small wooden chapel is surrounded by a fence, just like in ancient times – the sacred areas were separated from the profane. But what is this holy place, for whom is it sacred, part of which religion is it? We seem to find the answers to these questions when stepping over the doorstep. Inside, we see Christian symbols and icons and we understand that this is a chapel dedicated to St. George. And again, nothing unusual – it is one of the many chapels of this saint – very popular among the Orthodox Christians, as well as among the Catholics. But still, our sight finds something rather aberrant – a big marble relief of a horseman, which is built in the altar niche. Closer scrutiny reveals similar features to the image of the Christian saint, but what we don't find is the main character of St. George's iconography – the dragon killed by him – and we all know that St. George is a dragon slayer. Why not? We say to ourselves, this is a strange relief, but it is possible that the local population has depicted him in this way. On the right of the altar, a picture of an elderly couple is hung, and under it we read a short, handwritten story of the chapel.

For the archaeologists, this stone is important because they have found that it is a Thracian cult object and namely a depiction of the Thracian Horseman. But for those who worship and carry in their heart the connection with the lands of their ancestors, it is something more. From the inscription, which tells the century-old history of the chapel, we understand that the stone above the altar was found after a vision in a dream. This is a sign for what the ancients called *theophaneia* – divine appearance. The god (resp. the goddess) appears and gives to the mortals his image, so they may worship and call him through it.

The antiquity is far behind us; we live in the modern age, but our age doesn't start from nowhere. It has its beginning exactly in that ancient past, which for the archaeologists is represented only in finds, and for the historians, is part of their scientific material. This antiquity is still living and is among us; the divine appearance happens even nowadays, and the ancient gods are called and worshipped even in the present day. This example, which is not the only one, shows us that the Thracian faith and rituality continue to live on in the traditional belief of the Balkan peoples, in spite of their Christian or Muslim masks. Yes, there are changes – social, linguistic, and many more – but the essence of the faith, its connection with the sacred places of antiquity, its connection with the gods worshipped by the ancients – they are kept. The ancient deities remain gods of the rite; they are seen and heard – so, they are an object of hope, even nowadays. And even though their names can change, this doesn't affect their nature, which is called with the ritual acts, sacred words and the signs contained within them. An example of this is one ritual formula, an incantation, which is addressed to St. George, which again reveals the trust in a deity and not in a saint. This ritual formula is spoken over a woman whose children die because, it was believed, that the evening star takes them:

> Saint leading George headed, so he walks over the fields, over the field borders, so he went rainy frosty to his sister, Maria. And Saint Maria has recently given birth to a child and Saint George went to visit her and he knocked on the door:
> - Sister Maria, get up to open the door for me!
> - Brother George, I can't open the door, I just gave birth to a little child, the evening star can come and take my child.
> - Don't be afraid sister Maria, I will slaughter her with Wallachian knife, I will trample her with my horse (Wallachia is a part of modern Romania).
> - Brother George, she will turn into a millet grain, she'll hide in the horse's tack, she'll come and she'll take the child – we'll never see it again.
> - Don't be afraid sister Maria, while I'm here don't be afraid of anything.

And she got up and opened the door – and when she came back, she saw that the child was not in its bed. She went back to her brother and said to him:

> - Brother George, what did I tell you? That the evening star will come and steal it.

Saint George ate white cheese from Gergyovden, and he went to search for the child. On the road, he saw the blackberry bush and asked it:

> - Blackberry bush, you stay on the road, didn't you see the evening star with a child in her mouth?
> - I saw her not long ago – answered the blackberry bush – she just passed and was carrying it in her mouth.

- Be blessed, may, even if they cut your roots from your top, shall you be able to grow!

At another place along the road, he met the sycamore maple tree and asked it:

- Sycamore tree, you stay on the road, didn't you see the evening star with a child in her mouth?
- I saw her not long ago, Saint George – answered the sycamore tree – she just passed and was carrying it in her mouth.
- Be blessed – said Saint George – the earth and the sky will listen to you.

After that, he reached the olive tree.

- You stay on the road, olive tree, didn't you see the evening star with a small child in her mouth?
- I saw her not long ago, Saint George – answered the olive tree – she had already swallowed half of it, and the sea had swallowed half of her.
- Be also blessed olive tree, your oil will be poured in the sanctuary lamp and you'll shine in front of God (the icon)!

He walked a little bit more and he reached the sea, he called the evening star and she stopped in the middle of the sea. So he went to her and said to her:

- Evening star, spit out the child!
- How could I spit it out? – she answered – try to spit out the mother's milk with which your mother fed you, and then I'll spit out the child.

And, as he had eaten before that white cheese made on Gergyovden[1], he spat it out on his hand and said:

---

1   St. George's Day.

- Evening star, here I spit out my mother's milk, now you spit out the child!

Then she spat out the child on the hand of Saint George and said:

- Take it and bring it to your sister Maria, call a healer woman, she must take the herb maidenhair spleenwort[2] and she must make an incantation over the child, because its bones are crushed, because its blood is drunk. Incantations she must make with the herb maidenhair spleenwort, so that its blood fills up and its bones go back to their place.

I quoted this incantation because in it the notion of the saviour from the evil, who crushes it with his horse, is perfectly preserved. Nowadays, he is called among the Christians 'Saint George' – but in antiquity, the Thracian population gave him numerous local names and epithets. What is important in this case is that, regardless of the naming, the Horseman God is still 'seen' and called. But did only this god of the ancient Thracians keep his worship?

This is exactly the topic to which (as well as to the magical traditions in the traditional culture of the Balkan nations) my book, *Thracian Magic – Past & Present*, is dedicated. In it are discussed the images of Orpheus, Rhesos, Zalmoxis, the nymph Thrake, and others which the ancient Greeks described as Thracians proficient in the rites and in the mysteries of the gods. In the book are listed in detail numerous magical rites from the territory of Bulgaria, as well as from other Balkan countries. Passing through the calendar rituals, divine images from antiquity, which can be seen under the thin veil of Christianity and Islam, are highlighted. This book is planned as the first volume, and as for the ancient Thracians – the primordial is

---
2 Maidenhair spleenwort (Asplenium trichomanes).

the Great Goddess – so the text follows mainly her image in a number of ritual practices and explores their diachronic origin on the basis of ancient fragments and other data. I strongly recommend the book to everyone interested in the ancient world, contemporary magical folklore and the relicts within it. The book is available from Avalonia Books: http://avaloniabooks.co.uk/catalogue/hellenismos/thracian-magic

Witchcraft and the Monarchy

RICHARD SIMPSON

The English monarchy took an active interest in the occult sciences, with both direct and indirect participation by various historical royals, ranging from the level-headed to completely barking mad. Many witchcraft trials involving the monarchy were political, where 'witchcraft' and other similar terms were used as convenient props in political allegations playing on the paranoia of contemporary society. Witchcraft, in terms of English historical prosecution, was associated with the employment of supernatural mechanisms of doing harm – maleficium. Unfortunately, other terms came into play, such as sorcery, magic, conjuring, necromancy, and divination, which confused the issue. In many cases, practicing one particular art was taken to imply the performance of another, and classification as a 'white witch' or 'cunning folk' did not protect them from people who were still wary of their powers and thereby susceptible to accusations of maleficium.

Margaret Murray, in *God of the Witches*, linked the English monarchy directly with witchcraft, attributing the death of several kings to a pre-Christian 'Old Religion', including William II, Rufus. Rufus was killed by an arrow in the New Forest in 1100 AD, which Murray maintains was sacrificial at the hands of his friend, Walter Tyrel. Rufus was certainly a notoriously anti-clerical king; however, this did not imply that he was not Christian. On the contrary, he was a great supporter of Battle

Abbey, appointed his bitter enemy St. Anslem as Archbishop of Canterbury, and called a truce at the siege of Mayet out of respect for Easter. The defamation of Rufus' religious character was probably due to contemporary historians being generally clerical and who saw his demise as judgment for his antagonism of the Church. In fact, the night before his death, it was reported that Rufus was in high spirits, anticipating holding his Christmas court gathering at Poitiers, which was not the demeanour of someone expecting to be sacrificed the next day.

English monarchs schooled in Latin overcame ecclesiastical objections to occult texts by educating themselves – and their possession of the *Secreta Secretorum* evidenced the growing interest. This was an ancient Egyptian handbook containing advice on good health, physiognomy, alchemy, lapidary, astrology and divination. Henry III, Edward III, Henry VI, Edward IV and Henry VII all possessed copies – and Richard II owned the divination book, *Confessio Amantis*, which included extracts from the *Secreta* written at his request by John Gowan. This scholarly knowledge was put to practical use with a steady rise in incidents allegedly involving witchcraft in the acquisition of love and political power, and, by the late fourteenth century, these plots became a regular problem for the English monarchy. Acquired 'knowledge' by the elite, combined with the longstanding belief in local 'cunning folk' in the lower levels of society, provided a scenario where indulgence in magic and sorcery threaded through the complete social strata, resulting in most monarchs feeling threatened by witchcraft at some point. In fact, so seriously was the threat of witchcraft taken by the monarchy that cases were treated as treason and bypassed the usual ecclesiastical jurisdiction of Church courts that were responsible for the witchcraft prosecutions before the Witchcraft Statutes of 1542, 1563 and 1604.

Several cases illustrated the perceived link between treason and witchcraft. John Tannere was hanged for attempting to claim the crown through diabolical aid and asserting that he was Edward I's son. Thomas Burdett was convicted of treason in that he "worked and calculated by art magic, necromancy and astronomy the death" of Edward IV and the Prince of Wales. Thomas Southwell was tried for treason for using sorcery to seek the death of Henry VI. Similarly, Jane Shore and Elizabeth Woodville were tried, by an ecclesiastical court, for sorcery to harm Richard III. In 1496, there was an audacious and long-running conspiracy allegedly involving witchcraft to get Perkin Warbeck on the throne in place of Henry VII. Yorkists passed off Warbeck as Richard, Duke of York, one of Edward IV's children, who disappeared in the Tower of London. The story was believed by Edward IV's sister, and Warbeck subsequently attracted such support that it was hardly surprising that Henry VII responded with allegations of witchcraft. John Kendall, the Grand Prior of the Order of St. John of Rhodes, Sir John Thonge, and William Horsey, Archdeacon of London, were also accused of conspiracy against the family of Henry VII through the use of magical substances.

The translation of numerous Arab texts into Latin fuelled the growth of Neoplatonism, in particular, and encouraged the learned to accept the reality of the spiritual world – reinforcing the suspicion that anyone involved in magic was practicing witchcraft, thereby theologically underpinning witchcraft prosecutions. Neoplatonism hinged on the concept of spiritus mundi – the medium through which the stars influenced earthly occurrences and its manipulation, by magic, using 'good' demons – angels – as opposed to 'bad' demons. The concept of the demon provided a link between astrology and witchcraft, maleficent or beneficent, enabling the theologically trained prosecutor to establish cases against astrologers.

Two cases in particular illustrated the link between witchcraft and astrologers. Henry IV's widow, Queen Joan of Navarre, was arrested for treason by witchcraft along with her astrologer,

Friar Randolph, for attempting to destroy Henry V "by sorceyre and necromancye." Unfortunately for Joan, Randolph then also accused her of treason (sparing himself execution) and she was gaoled for three years. Eleanor Cobham, second wife of Henry V's brother, was arrested for using weather magic to endanger Henry VI and using sorcery to establish when the king would die in order to further the advancement of her husband to the crown. As she had been her husband's mistress during his first marriage, she was further charged with sorcery to gain his love, annul his marriage and marry her. Lady Cobham was fortunate and escaped gaol, whilst accomplices Marger Jourdemayne, 'The Witch of Eye', was burnt and Roger Bolinbroke, astrologer, was hanged, drawn and quartered for treason.

With astrology, English monarchs faced a dilemma as they needed to balance the advantages of gleaning the future against theological objections; however, the sheer exclusivity of being able to use an astrologer combined with the power to deal with objectors overcame any opposition. The Tudors, especially, encouraged astrology, with Henry VII, Henry VIII, Edward VI and Elizabeth I all consulting astrologers. Significantly, as head of the English Church, Henry VIII also prevented his bishops from censuring astrology, whilst exhibiting a certain hypocrisy about the distinction between astrology and divination – both were designated princely activities in the *Secreta Secretorum*. Divination particularly worried Henry VIII, especially where it concerned the length of the monarch's reign or royal succession, and resulted in high-profile trials of the Duke of Buckingham (1521), Sir William Neville (1532), Lord Hungerford (1540), and Henry Nevill (1546). However, some light may be shed if we consider Buckingham, in particular. Not only was he descended from the same bloodline as Edward III, but he had been informed by a conjuring priest, Nicholas Hopkins, in 1514, that Henry VIII would have no heir and Buckingham would inherit the crown.

Even royal astrologers could be seen by certain sectors of society as dabbling in witchcraft. During the accession of Elizabeth I, John Dee, astrologer and mathematician, was asked to determine the optimum coronation date by astrology, despite having been investigated in 1553 by the Star Chamber for trying to kill Queen Mary by poison or magic. Henceforth, he acted as Astrologer Royal, counselling Elizabeth on the best way to cope with perceived attempts to assassinate her through magic. Dee maintained a library on all aspects of magic, including continental witchcraft, and, from 1584, dabbled in alchemy and attempted to raise angels. His house was sacked at one point by a mob suspecting him of dabbling in witchcraft, and the subsequent persistent rumour of witchcraft drove him to petition James I, unsuccessfully, to be cleared of the accusation of being a "conjuror, or caller, or invocator of devils."

The accession of Elizabeth I led to widespread paranoia about Catholic plots to topple the Protestant regime, and the Privy Council went to great lengths to investigate sorcery cases. Sir Anthony Fortescue, who was in allegiance with the nephews of Cardinal Pole, Mary Queen of Scots, the French and Spanish Ambassadors and two conjurors, John Prestall and Edmund Cosyn, allegedly prophesied that Elizabeth would die naturally with the help of a "wicked spryte". This increased paranoia, and when Mary Queen of Scots was imprisoned, a special team of investigators, under the direction of the Earl of Shrewsbury, was employed to detect conjurors. In 1562, Elizabeth had the Countess of Lennox imprisoned on a charge of alleged sorcery and witchcraft in order to stop Lennox's son, Lord Darnley, marrying Mary Queen of Scots. Later, in 1583, there was a further alleged high-profile Catholic conspiracy involving Francis Throckmorton, Baron Pagil, Sir George Hastings, and Sir Thomas Hanmer and "Ould Birtles, the great devil, Darnally the sorcerer, Maude Twogoode, enchantresse, and the oulde witche of Ramsbury."

Accounts of monarchic involvement in magical practices are dogged by conflicting allegations by contemporary historians according to their political allegiance. Henry IV was alleged to have handed Parliament a magical scroll found in the chest of Richard Magdalene, Richard II's priest, resulting in the arrest of all Richard II's counsellors. This account was related by Thomas Walsingham, a Lancastrian, who also alleged that Richard II, a Plantagenet, was a tyrant prone to association with sorcerers and prophets encouraging ambition to become a Holy Roman Emperor. However, no record can be found of the event taking place in contemporary administrative documents. It must be said, however, that an inventory of Richard II's royal treasures revealed a number of 'quadrants' used in astronomical calculations, but it is debatable as to whether they were sophisticated enough for astrology, and a search of his Westminster Abbey tomb by Dean Stanley in 1871, found objects that "had doubtless been put there as a precaution against witchcraft." Richard II commissioned a book on divination in 1391, but there is no evidence that he used it, and it may just have been part of his library as an enthusiastic collector of literature, including Geoffrey Chaucer's *The Franklin's Tale*, which describes the working of magic. Richard II was not alone in commissioning books on the magic arts, with Henry VII obtaining several astrology and geomancy textbooks, including *Tabulae Glowantriae injudicus artis geomancie*.

The battles of the English monarch against the perceived threat of witchcraft were characterised by the justification of God on their side. John Wagstaff, in 1669, asserted that witchcraft was defined to maintain the charismatic pretences of heathen rulers, and this was perpetuated by their medieval and early-modern counterparts. To some extent this was true, as the period 1327 to 1485, from late Plantagenet through Lancaster and York to Tudor, was characterized by the loss and seizures of thrones, with the exception of Henry V. The Duke of Orleans accused Henry IV (Lancaster) of obtaining the throne from Richard II

(Plantagenet) by witchcraft as opposed to divine right. Richard III usurped Edward V, justified by God's will, on the basis that Edward IV had a pre-contract of matrimony with one Eleanor Butler and therefore lived "sinfully and in damnable adultery" with Elizabeth, his queen – and the marriage had been made by the sorcery and witchcraft of the Duchess of Bedford, Elizabeth's mother. Divine right even extended beyond the person of the monarch, as experienced by Henry IV's campaigns against Owen Glendower in Wales. These were impeded by inclement weather allegedly raised using witchcraft by Franciscan friars favourable to the Welsh, and countered by the assertion that the weather was divine, as the English had no right to Wales. The sum value of these artificial lines of succession was the concept of divine right becoming a fixture of the office of monarch, as opposed to the monarch's person.

Although political witchcraft trials were a common feature of the English monarchy, the accusation of diabolism was rare. The latter fourteenth and early fifteenth centuries experienced an increase in trials for diabolism due in part to the inquisitional procedure, which did away with penalties for the accuser who failed to substantiate his charges. It is a misconception that the continental notion of a pact with the Devil, as a basis for prosecution, arrived only with James I. Edward I's treasurer, Walter Langton, Bishop of Coventry, was charged before the Pope with having formed a pact with the Devil but was acquitted with the support of Roger Mortimer, protector of the young Edward III, who tried to frame the murdered Edward II's brother, Edmund, Earl of Kent, with making a pact with the Devil to obtain the crown.

A considerable number of perceived threats to the monarchy involved love and image magic, which had been forbidden under the designation of invultuation by Henry I. John de Nottingham, a necromancer, was charged with trying to kill Edward II and the Prior of Coventry with image magic. Edward II's obsessive attachment to Piers Gaveston was attributed to sorcery, as it was an accepted normal practice of ingratiating oneself with royalty in France – Edward III's mistress, Alice Perrers was charged with both gaining the monarch's affections and causing his madness using magical arts. Both Cardinal Wolsey and Thomas Cromwell were alleged to have used magic rings to secure the favour of Henry VIII, as (supposedly) did Anne Boleyn.

It is possible that the use of image magic during the Tudors prompted references to it in the Witchcraft Statutes, as there were two incidents which were taken very seriously. A wax baby with two pins in its head was found in a London churchyard in 1538, with the face of the future Edward VI – possibly prompting the reference to images in Henry VIII's 1542 Witchcraft Act. In 1578, there was uncovered evidence of a plot to kill Elizabeth I and two of her advisors by image magic; however, no suspects were arrested – but the following year, a group of Windsor witches were interrogated for allegedly using image magic in the form of a bewitched puppet.

A form of magic officially recognised by the Crown was the cure of the 'royal touch', which specifically pertained to the King's Evil – an inflammation of the lymph glands. Viewed as a mystical power coming with the office of monarch, the ability to cure the Evil was seen as an indication of the right to the English throne and symbolic of dynastic legitimacy. The Church had long monopolised the power of healing by faith, and it appears that the monarchy 'commandeered' some of this faculty to raise itself to a mystical level. In fact, the royal touch became more of a political tool than an altruistic gift, with Elizabeth I using it to rubbish the papal bull of excommunication, Charles I for Royalist propaganda during the Civil War, Charles II to justify the Restoration and the Stuarts in Jacobite propaganda after 1688. The tradition was initiated by Edward the Confessor and grew in popularity down the different lineages of monarchy, peaking at 8,577 'touches' in the twelve months of 1683, during the reign of Charles II.

Curiously, for such a divine power, James I exercised the royal touch reluctantly in the name of tradition, as he regarded it as superstitious, and eventually it declined in use after 1688, with an absolute refusal by William II, although Queen Anne did occasionally consent to apply it. In contradiction, traditional cunning folk had long used the power of touch in their healing rituals – and were harassed with allegations of witchcraft as a result. It has been suggested that perhaps the authorities viewed the ability to cure the King's Evil as a form of royal monopoly, thereby artificially maintaining mystification of the monarchy, as illustrated in the case of Presbyterian minister Thomas Rosewell, who was tried for treason in 1684 for casting doubt on the reality of royal healing power.

Pre-Reformation, witchcraft prosecutions had mainly been left to the Church, except in treason cases. However, with the fusion of learned and popular belief, there was increasing pressure to formulate laws against witchcraft, especially when Henry VIII became head of the Church of England – what was formerly a crime against the Church, became a crime against the king. This marked an important stepping stone in the formulation of the 1542 Witchcraft Act, allowing secular prosecution of alleged maleficium.

On becoming King of England, James I strengthened the Witchcraft Statutes in 1604, a principal feature of which being that mere contact with the Devil or a wicked spirit now became a capital offence (as opposed to the previous necessary evidence of maleficium) and established the continental idea of pacts and Devil-worship in English law. Significantly, the practice of beneficent 'white magic' also became a capital offence on second conviction. Under James I's rule, there were 37 capital witchcraft convictions, only twenty of which were for murder – hence, seventeen would have escaped under Elizabeth. Some have maintained that the introduction of continental ideas in the 1604 Act helped undermine the credibility of witchcraft prosecutions and therefore speeded an end to them; however, if so, its effect was very slow, as the infamous witch-hunter Mathew Hopkins relied heavily on James I's tome *Daemonologie* through his short but bloody career.

James I's original intention in writing *Daemonologie* was to counter the opinions of Reginald Scot and German physician, Johann Weyer – both of whom thought that those believing themselves to be witches were deluded. James' position, on accession to the English throne, as both head of the Church and head of state, significantly increased the influence of *Daemonologie* on witch-hunting, especially in terms of evidence, where he held that the witch's mark and swimming were proof of guilt. However, it must be said that *Daemonologie* was only one of a string of books that James authored and may just have been written to satisfy his desire to be seen as a philosopher king and satisfy his religious, mystical and political pretensions, as his only reference to witchcraft, outside *Daemonologie*, is in *Basilikon Doron*: "There are some horrible crimes that ye are bound in conscience never to forgive: such as witchcraft."

During the Stuart dynasty, science and reason rose to the fore, whilst serious belief in witchcraft and heresy declined. James I's beliefs in the continental concept of demonology, after conversations with Lutherans and Niels Hemmingsen, had a significant impact in Scotland, where previously witches were prosecuted under the doctrine of maleficium. The North Berwick trials, particularly, appear to have stimulated James' interest in witchcraft, if only because the objective had been to kill him and allegedly involved his cousin, the Earl of Bothwell. Such was his interest that he took a prominent part in both the interrogation and prosecution to the extent of trying to have 'not guilty' verdicts reversed. He also took a personal interest in the 1597 St. Andrew's trial, where again there was an alleged plot to drown him – and in 1620, a schoolmaster named Peacock was examined and tortured for practicing magic to bewitch James I's judgment. James I, it would appear, only took witch-hunting to extreme lengths when he felt personally threatened, but one may argue that he had great justification to be paranoid about real or imagined threats to his royal person – his father, Darnley, was murdered, two of his regents were shot, and another, the Earl of Mar, died within a year of 'natural causes'.

James, confusingly, occupied an ambiguous position on witchcraft, maintaining that the innocent should not be condemned, yet asserting it a sin not to convict the guilty. His accession to the English throne appears to have reduced witch-hunting fervour, and total prosecutions actually dropped below the Elizabethan level. James revoked all witch-hunting commissions, as he was of the opinion that citizens were not properly safeguarded against false accusations, and on two occasions personally intervened to remove false charges. A number of fraudulent witch trials, such as Lancashire, 1612, and Staffordshire, 1620, led to the gradual onset of scepticism, and in 1616, in Leicester, he even compelled a boy to retract accusations which had cost the lives of nine women. Sometimes his scepticism was so great that it descended into outright flippancy. In response to a question, he once declared that he was "busy with hunting of witches, prophets, puritans, dead cats and hares," and on another occasion James ended a woman's 'trance' by ripping off her bedclothes. According to courtier Lucy Aitken, "The frequency of such forged possessions wrought such an alteration upon the judgment of King James that he, receding from what he had written in his *Daemonologie* grew first diffident of, and then flatly to deny, the workings of witches and devils as falsehoods and delusions."

The accession of Charles I saw a steep decline in prosecutions. Under Charles, there were only six executions, with the king exhibiting the same trend of scepticism as his father. Again, he took a personal interest in proceedings, particularly the 1633 Lancashire witch scare, and, aided by his personal physician,

Harvey, exposed it as a fabrication. Harvey, it appears, was as active as the king in exposing fraud – in one particular incident, he cut a witch's toad familiar in two to discover that it was just a toad. However, this did not remove allegations of witchcraft completely from his court. During the Civil War, the ability of Wardour Castle to hold out against the Royalists was attributed to the witchcraft of Robert Barham, a Puritan preacher.

Persecution of occult practices was finally laid to rest with the 1735 Witchcraft Act, under George II – and may it RIP. No longer was it a capital offence to be a witch but rather an offence to pretend to have occult powers. Seemingly a step in the right direction, it brought instead a whole new era of persecution, but that is another story.

Witchcraft before Wicca

MICHAEL HOWARD

Today the popular image of witchcraft in the mass media and in books and magazines is largely defined by Wicca. This was a form of Neo-Pagan witchcraft created by a retired civil servant, Gerald Brosseau Gardner (1884–1964), in the1940s. Gardner was initiated into a coven in the New Forest 70 years ago, in 1939, and Wicca is now established worldwide as a postmodern, Neo-Pagan 'nature religion' with a spiritual emphasis on goddess-worship. Modern witchcraft, however, did not begin with Gardner, and it has a hidden history before Wicca. From the 1800s onwards, there were several revivals of witchcraft in Britain based on historical precedents. These drew on the recorded beliefs and practices of the medieval witch cult and rural cunning people or folk magicians, revivals of classical Paganism, ceremonial magic, diabolism, and Neo-Druidic sources and were also influenced by Rosicrucianism and Freemasonry. Today, such forms of pre-Wiccan traditional witchcraft are variously known as 'Traditional Craft', 'The Nameless Arte', and 'The Crooked Path'.

There is plenty of evidence from historical sources, folklore accounts, court cases and, later, newspaper reports in Britain of the activities of so-called cunning folk and other practitioners of magic who were popularly regarded as witches. In popular terminology, and belief, they were variously known as 'white witches', 'wizards', 'sorcerers', 'conjurors', 'pellars', 'plant-readers' (astrologers), and 'hedge doctors' (herbalists). These magical practitioners operated widely in both the rural and urban areas of the British Isles and were consulted by all levels of society, from farm labourers to the owners of large country estates and the wealthy middle-class in towns.

These so-called witches offered a wide range of services to their clients. They were popularly believed to possess the second sight (or the ability to foresee the future), exorcise ghosts and banish spirits and poltergeists, cast spells to attract love and money, locate lost or stolen property and missing people using divination or by consulting spirits, and heal the sick using the laying on of hands or herbal remedies. Most importantly, as far as their clients were concerned, they could counter the malefic spells cast by so-called 'grey' or 'black' witches. In some cases, the cunning men or wise-women even acted for the general population and the authorities as unofficial witch-finders. However, all these types of witches were believed to be able to cure and curse, hex and heal.

Although there are obvious similarities with some of the modern magical practices carried out by Wiccans, most of the methods and techniques used by the old-time witches bear little resemblance to those used by the Neo-Pagan witches who appear today in the press or on television. Often the cunning folk practised dual-faith observance, and the charms, amulets, prayers and incantations they used invoked Jesus, the Virgin Mary, the Trinity, and the company of saints.

Many of the grimoires used by witches and the practitioners of folk magic also contained Judeo-Christian symbolism.

Christian symbolism was used in folk magic rituals involving psychic protection, counter-magic and healing. Many of the old Pagan charms were Christianised, and some of the saints took on the earlier attributes of Pagan gods and goddesses – sacred springs previously dedicated to goddesses, for instance, were re-dedicated either to the Virgin Mary or to female saints, such as Winifrede or Bride. Healing charms replaced the names of Pagan deities such as Woden, Loki, and Thor with those of Jesus, the Virgin Mary, and the Holy Ghost. Psalms were used for magical purposes as spells, and they still are in some modern traditional witchcraft circles. With the coming of the new religion of Christianity and the suppression of the ancient Paganism, objects such as crucifixes, saints' medallions, the host, and holy water were widely used by folk magicians because they were believed to possess virtue or magical energy and inherent healing power.

Some modern traditional witches still follow dual-faith observance, using the psalms for magical purposes, working with the company of saints and employing Christian imagery, symbolism and liturgy, often in a heretical and subversive way. This is akin to similar practices that can be found in vodou, hoodoo, Santeria, Macumba, ju-ju and obeah in North and South America and Africa. In common with the witches and cunning folk of the past, the modern traditional witch can also both cure and curse as the need arises.

A considerable amount of the old Paganism survived in the popular belief in the 'Good Folk' or fairies. There are many historical examples of witches and cunning folk travelling into a hollow hill or mountain or visiting a prehistoric burial mound to meet the 'Queen of Elfane' ('elf home' or Faeryland). Some mortals entered into 'faery marriages' with so-called demon lovers, and in return they were instructed in healing and divination techniques, herbalism and given the second sight. These gifts were passed on down through the generations, such as in the case of the famous hereditary 'fairy doctors' or physicians of Myddfai in South Wales, who received their herbal knowledge from a local 'Lady of the Lake'.

This knowledge of magical charms, herbal remedies and secret plant lore was passed down in families either orally or by the medium of written texts. Many of the cunning folk and witches of the eighteenth and nineteenth centuries were literate people, and several of the most famous cunning men or wizards were doctors, school teachers or even clergymen. Grimoires such as the medieval *Key of Solomon* and books on magic, fortune-telling and astrology were freely available. They could be purchased by mail-order from booksellers in London who specialised in the occult and pornography. In the nineteenth century, several astrological and occult magazines were also published and gained a wide popular readership. There is also evidence of handwritten grimoires or magical manuals known as 'black books' circulating among witches and magicians. These were similar to the modern Wiccan *Book of Shadows*, except that instead of Neo-Pagan seasonal rituals, they contained spells, charms and recipes for herbal remedies.

Because it was widely believed that certain of the cunning folk could 'smell out' malefic practitioners of the magical arts, several of the famous cunning men were credited with being able to locate or even control the witches living in their neighbourhood. It was only a short step from this belief to the idea that some of these 'masters of witches' or 'witch masters' might secretly be the leaders of the local coven. According to Victorian folk tales, such covens or covines met in the remote countryside at the full moon to worship Old Hornie (the Devil) and practise their evil spells against God-fearing folk who were tucked up in bed. These may have been romanticised accounts, but there is evidence that solitary cunning men and wise-women did meet up with others in their locality to practice magic, swap recipes for spells, and exchange occult knowledge. It is logical that to avoid prying eyes, such clandestine gatherings would be held at lonely spots in the countryside and on the nights when the moon gave the most light.

What of traditional witchcraft today and the differences between it and modern Wicca? Unlike the average Wiccan, the traditional witch prefers to work outdoors rather than in a cosy, centrally heated, suburban sitting room. For that reason, they do not go skyclad (naked) – instead preferring robes or cloaks with hoods. This is why traditional groups are sometimes called robed covens. As one would expect from the fact that they usually work outdoors, the genius loci or 'spirit of the place', the wights or earth spirits of the land, are very important in their magical workings.

The mystical concept of the enchanted or sacred landscape is important because, although all forms of traditional witchcraft have similarities, they also relate to the region they are practised in, and this creates local differences in practice and belief.

Traditional witches regard themselves as the human stewards or guardians of ancient sites such as stone circles, standing stones, and burial mounds. They will frequently work their rites on or near the prehistoric trackways that mark the 'spirit paths', 'ghost roads', 'corpse roads', or ley-lines that crisscross the British countryside between these natural power centres.

While they recognise the magical power inherent in the fauna and flora, traditional witches are less likely to be sentimental about the environment than Wiccans. Traditionalists do recognise that nature can be 'red in tooth and claw' and that natural laws are based on the 'survival of the fittest'.

Unlike Wiccan covens that are ruled by a high priestess, with her high priest as consort, and where initiation is always male to female or female to male, traditional covines are led by a male leader known as the Magister, Master or Devil. He can initiate both men and women into the Craft. This is because sexual polarity is not such an important aspect of Traditional Craft and for that reason many traditionalist groups are known as 'knowledge covines'. The Magister sometimes has a male deputy called the Summoner who is responsible for organising the dates, times and places for the meetings. The female leader is known variously as the Magistra, Mistress, Maid, Lady, Dame, or Queen of the Sabbat. Some groups also have a Verdelet or Green Man whose task is to teach the other coveners the secrets of the magical powers and healing properties of herbs, trees, and plants. Other roles within the covine can include the Scribe, Seer, and the Mistress of the Robes.

Within the operative or magical practices of traditional witchcraft can be found the concept of spirit flight (astral projection) at the Witches' Sabbath, sometimes using the unguentum sabbati or 'flying ointment' made from narcotic plants. Techniques of psychic vision, trance, mediumship, 'true dreaming' and spirit-possession are also used to contact the Otherworld in ways that are allied to ethnic forms of shamanism. Elementals and spirits are summoned, and there is communion with the realm of Faerie, the use of familiars, fetches (the witch's astral double) and spirit-guides, shapeshifting into animal form, divination, necromancy, and wort cunning (healing with herbs and plants).

Traditional witches approach divinity in either a duo-theistic of polytheistic way. The deities or spirits revered in Traditional Craft are the 'twilight gods' – chthonic ones associated with the powers of life and death, creation and destruction. They are also often the ones that orthodox religion describes as the powers of darkness. This is why, historically, the witch has always been regarded as a social outcast and a religious rebel. The witch goddess in traditional witchcraft has both a bright and a dark aspect. For that reason, she is sometimes associated with the waxing and waning of the moon or the full and dark moon, and also with fate and the underworld. She can be personified mythologically as Dame Hecate, Diana, Frau Holda, Habondia, Lilith, and Titania or the Queen of the Faeries.

The horned god of the witches is also dual-faced, as the Lord of the Wildwood and the Green Man in his summer aspect, and the Lord of the Wild Hunt and Lord of Death in winter. In mythic terms, he can be represented as Herne, Wayland, Puck or Robin Goodfellow, Tubal-Cain, Siwanus, Lucifer or Azazel, and Oberon or the King of Eves. He appears in animal form as a stag, bull, goat, ram or a black dog. Some traditional witches prefer not to associate their deities with any ancient mythology. Instead, they refer to them obliquely in generic terms as the Old Ones, the Old Lad and Old Lass, the Old Man and the Old Woman, the Lord and Lady, the Horned One, Old Hornie, the Devil, the Old Dame, or even just Him and Her.

Although a few traditional and hereditary witches (those belonging to a family tradition) have come out of the shadows in recent years, they are far more reluctant than Wiccans to seek publicity. They are not likely to appear on daytime television wearing crushed velvet robes, carrying a ram's skull on a stick, waving swords and covered in occult bling. They usually live in rural areas, and they often look surprisingly normal, wear ordinary clothes and blend into the background. Because they possess a fund of knowledge about the constellations, fauna and flora, ancient and local history, and the weather, ordinary people may just think they have a keen interest in country matters, nature and folklore.

Wicca obviously attracts many people today, especially those seeking a trendy green political form of spirituality that worships nature. However, those who follow modern traditional witchcraft do not regard themselves as 'nature-worshippers', or even as 'Pagans'. Many do not believe that the Craft is a religion, per se – and certainly not a 'nature religion'. Instead, they regard it as a mystery cultus offering an ancient heritage of forbidden wisdom and occult (hidden) knowledge. It is a mystical path that leads to spiritual enlightenment and, ultimately, to gnosis and union with the Godhead. As such, it represents a bright lantern shining in the dark for those dedicated seekers who want to contact the ancient mysteries in the modern world.

Michael Howard was the editor of *The Cauldron* witchcraft magazine since 1976. He is the author of 30 books, and his latest publications are: *Witches and Wizards* (Three Hands Press, USA, 2009), *Wicca: From Gerald Gardner to the Present* (Llewellyn,

USA, 2010), *West Country Witches* (Three Hands Press, USA, 2010), and *Children of Cain: A Study of Modern Traditional Witches* (Three Hands Press, USA, 2011).

Mike Howard died in 2015.
Published by kind permission of the estate of Micheal Howard.

The Spirit of the Woods: The Welsh Tradition of Myrddin/Merlin

AUGUST HUNT

MYRDDIN OF AVALON

Who was Merlin – or, rather, what was Merlin?

This question has intrigued and vexed countless students of the Arthurian tradition for centuries. Was he someone who panicked and ran away from the Battle of Arfderydd? Who lost his sanity in the battle and lived like a wild beast in the woods? Had he really been a great bard of the chieftain Gwenddolau? If he were a madman, by what mechanism did his insane pronouncements become recognized as prophecies? Why was he also called Llallogan or Llallawg? Why was he dealt a triple sacrificial death akin to that meted out to the god Lleu (Gaulish Lugos, Irish Lugh) in the Welsh *Mabinogion*?

These questions are important in and of themselves, of course. But for our purposes, they take on a more profound significance. When we answer them in an objective way, can we say definitively that Merlin had belonged to a class of Druidic priests? Or that he had performed some vital function for such a priesthood?

In Geoffrey of Monmouth's *History of the Kings of Britain*, Merlin, the Welsh Myrddin, is associated with Amesbury's Stonehenge on Salisbury Plain and with Mount Killaraus (= Killare, next to the Hill of Uisneach, the centre of Ireland);

while in Geoffrey's *Life of Merlin*, the great sage is placed atop a mountain in the Scottish Caledonian Wood.

Fragments of the Life of St. Kentigern tell of a madman/prophet named Lailoken, who is explicitly identified with Merlin and who is found on a 'rock' at Mellodonor (modern Molindinar Burn) within sight of Glasgow and at Drumelzier (modern Dunmeller) in the Scottish Borders. Lailoken is said to have been buried near Drumelzier.

Before Geoffrey introduced Merlin into the Arthurian saga by substituting him for Ambrosius of Dinas Emrys (a hillfort in Gwynedd), Wales, and of Wallop, Hampshire (see below), the madman/prophet had divided his time between Carwinelow, the fort of his lord Gwenddolau, near Longtown in Liddesdale (known now as the Moat of Liddel), nearby Arthuret (the scene of the Battle of Arfderydd, in which his lord was slain and he went mad), the Lowland Caledonian Wood with its mountain, and the court of King Rhydderch Hen/Hael. Rhydderch belongs at Dumbarton in Strathclyde, although Geoffrey makes him a Cumbrian king.

MYRDDIN'S MOUNTAIN

In Geoffrey, the Caledonian mountain of Merlin remains unnamed. This is unfortunate, in that by finding this mountain we might learn a great deal more about Merlin's identity. And, incidentally, we would have a much firmer fix on the location of Arthur's seventh battle, which occurred in the Caledonian Wood.

Merlin's Caledonian Wood mountain is mentioned in one other source: the thirteenth-century French verse romance by Guillaume le Clerc entitled *Fergus of Galloway*. The Fergus romance is distinguished by the author's knowledge of Scottish geography. To quote from Cedric E. Pickford in *Arthurian Literature in the Middle Ages*:

"His [Guillaume's] Scottish geography is remarkably accurate ... In the whole range of Arthurian romance, there is no instance of a more detailed, more realistic geographical setting."

The modern translator of Fergus, the late D.D.R. Owen, has made similar remarks on this romance. The notes and synopses in his translation also remind the reader that various elements of the Fergus mountain episode were adapted from Chretien's *Yvain* and *Perceval*, and the *Continuations of* the latter.

But it remains true that only Fergus actually names Merlin's mountain and purports to give us directions on how to get there. The hero Fergus starts his journey to the mountain not, as Nikolai Tolstoy (in his *The Quest for Merlin*) claims, at the Moat of Liddel, where Merlin fought and fled in madness, but at Liddel Castle at Newcastleton in Liddesdale. Tolstoy uses 1) Guillaume's directions and the placement of King Rhydderch at Dumbarton; 2) Merlin's affinity with the stag in Geoffrey's *Life of Merlin*; 3) the incorrect positioning of Merlin's Galabes springs (see below); and 4) the great height of the hill to select Hart Fell at the head of Annandale as Merlin's mountain.

There are marked problems with each of these guidelines used by Tolstoy. Firstly, the directions given are incredibly vague and hence can be used to chart a course from the Moat of Liddel to just about anywhere:

"[Fergus] comes riding along the edge of a mighty forest ... Fergus comes onto a very wide plain between two hills. On he rode past hillocks and valleys until he saw a mountain appear that reached up to the clouds and supported the entire sky ..."

Secondly, Fergus' mountain is given two names, neither of which matches that of Hart Fell: Noquetran (variants Nouquetran,

Noquetrant) and 'Black Mountain'. The latter is obviously a poetic designation only, the primary name being Noquetran.

And thirdly, there is no edifice of any kind atop or on the flanks of Hart Fell which could have been referred to as 'Merlin's Chapel'. As described in the Fergus romance, this edifice must be an ancient chambered cairn. Such monuments are often associated with Arthurian characters.

The hill-name Noquetran is obviously a Norman French attempt at a Gaelic hill-name, with the first component being cnoc, in English 'knock' – 'hill'. As the French render the English 'bank' as banque, and 'check' as cheque, cnoc/knock became noque-.

The secret to correctly interpreting the -tran component of Noquetran lies in a closer examination of Professor Owen's notes on the Fergus romance. For lines 773-93, he writes:

> "This adventure [of the Noquetran] is largely developed from elements in *C.II* [*the Second Continuation* of Chretien's *Perceval*]. There, Perceval fights and defeats a black knight in mysterious circumstances. Earlier, he had found a fine horn hanging by a sash from a castle door. On it he gave three great blasts, whereupon he was challenged by a knight, the horn's owner, whose shield was emblazoned with a white lion. Perceval vanquished this Chevalier du Cor and sent him to surrender to Arthur. At his castle he learned of a high mountain, the Mont Dolorous, on whose summit was a marvellous pillar ... fashioned long ago by Merlin."

For lines 4460 ff, Owen writes:

> "Mont Dolorous, which also appears in *C.II* (see note above to *C.II*, lines 773-93), is here associated with Melrose and is probably to be identified with the nearby Eildon Hills ..."

In the Fergus romance, the Noquetran episode comes first. The horn hangs from a white lion (cf. the lion on the knight's shield in the *Perceval Continuation*) in the Noquetran chapel, where Merlin had spent many a year. In front of the chapel is a bronze giant, apparently a statue, whose arms are broken off by Fergus, causing the giant's great bronze hammer to fall to the ground. Later in the romance, Fergus goes to the Dolorous Mountain or the Eildons and encounters there a club-wielding giant in the Castle of the Dark Rock (reminiscent of the 'Black Mountain' name applied to the Noquetran).

As it happens, the Eildons are noteworthy for having three major ancient monuments atop two of their three hills. On the Eildon North Hill is the largest hillfort in Scotland, the probable oppidum of the Selgovae tribe. Here also is a Roman signal station.

But on Eildon Mid Hill is a large Bronze Age cairn. This ancient burial mound is situated on the southwest flank of Eildon Mid Hill, about 30m below the summit, at a height of some 395m OD. It has been much robbed and now appears as a low, irregular mound of stones, about 15m in diameter, from which a few boulders protrude to indicate the possible former presence of a cist.

More remarkable was the presence below the cairn of a group of seven bronze socketed axes. These axes are now in the Royal Museum of Scotland.

This group of seven socketed axes was found in 1982 on the lower western slopes of Eildon Mid Hill, Ettrick and Lauderdale District, Borders Region. Although recovered from redeposited soil, the axes probably represent a hoard of the Ewart Park phase of the late Bronze Age. The find reinforces what appears to be a significant local concentration of contemporary metalwork around the Eildon Hills.

In view of their discovery in redeposited soil, we cannot be absolutely certain how the axes were originally deposited.

However, their number, their proximity and their similar condition all suggest that they came from a hoard, probably close to their eventual find-spot. Whether the seven axes recovered in August 1982 comprised the whole hoard remains uncertain. On the other hand, it is possible, though less likely, that more than one separate deposit was originally involved.

These bronze axes immediately remind us of the bronze hammer in the Fergus romance's account of Merlin's Chapel. This being so, I would see in the name 'Noquetran' or Noquetrant a Gaelic cnoc or anglicized 'knock', plus one of the following:

G. *dreann* – grief, pain (cf. Irish *drean*: sorrow, pain, melancholy);

or

G. *treana, treannadh* – lamentation, wailing.

In other words, Noquetran is merely a Gaelic rendering of the Old French 'Mont Dolorous' – the famous Dolorous Mountain of Arthurian romance!

The bronze hammer Fergus causes to be dropped near Merlin's Chapel on the Noquetran is a folk memory of a bronze socketed axe being deposited on the slope below the Eildon Mid Hill cairn or, more probably, of such an axe being found on the site prior to Guillaume le Clerc's writing of the Fergus romance. Merlin's Noquetran chapel is the Eildon Mid Hill Bronze Age cairn.

Melrose Mountain, Black Mountain and Castle of the Dark Rock are all designations for the Eildons. The hill-name 'Eildon' is found in 1130 as Eldunum and in 1150 as Eldune. This could be (according to the Scottish place-name expert, Watson) O.E. aelet + dunas, 'fire hills', or G. *aill*, 'a rock, cliff', plus O.E. dun, 'a hill'. The Fergus romance's 'Castle of the Dark Rock' (Li Chastiaus de la Roce Bise) may stand for the hillfort on Eildon North Hill, with Eildon being perceived as composed of *aill*, rock, plus not dun, 'hill', but instead O.E. dun, 'a colour partaking of brown and black'; M.E. dunne, donne, 'dark-coloured': Ir. *Dunn*, 'a dun colour': Wel. *dwn, dun*, 'swarthy, dusky': G. *Donn*, 'brown-coloured'.

So why were the Eildons identified with the Dolorous Mountain/Noquetran? The answer may lie in part with Nikolai Tolstoy's astute observation that the lion Fergus thinks should be roaming over the mountaintop, but which he finds inside the 'chapel', is an error or substitution for the god Lugos (Wel. *Lleu*, Ir. *Lugh*). In Welsh, Lleu's name could sometimes be spelled Llew, and the latter is the normal spelling for the Welsh word for 'lion'. Merlin's associations with Lleu will be discussed below. For now, suffice it to say that the Dolorous Mountain got its name because the divine name Lugos or Lugh was at some point wrongly linked to the Latin lugeo, 'to mourn, to lament, bewail'. Such mistakes in language could easily have occurred when going from Celtic to Old French. It may even be that in preferring lugeo to Lugos, a Pagan religious secret was being disguised and thus protected.

The Dolorous Mountain is then, properly, 'Lugos Mountain'. And the Lugos/Lugh/Lleu mountain in particular is Eildon Mid Hill, the highest of the Eildons, with its Bronze Age cairn. Such an identification of the Dolorous Mountain has implications for the Dolorous Garde of Lancelot, especially given that Lancelot himself is a late literary manifestation of the god Lugh, something first discussed long ago by the noted Arthurian scholar, Roger Sherman Loomis. I have parsed Lancelot of the Lake as *Llwch* (the Welsh spelling for the Irish god Lugh) + *lamh-calad* (Ir.) / *llaw-caled* (Wel.), that is, 'Lugh of the Hard-hand'.

We know of five Lugh forts in Britain – four known and one unlocated. Of the former, there is Dinas Dinlle in Gwynedd, Loudoun in East Ayrshire, Luguvalium or Carlisle in Cumbria, and Lleuddiniawn or 'Lothian', 'Land of the Fort of Lugh'. Din Eidyn, modern Edinburgh, the capital of Lothian, preserves the name of Lugh's mother in Irish tradition, Eithne. Luguvalium has been interpreted as containing a personal name, Lugovalos,

'Lugos-strong', but I believe this name is instead a descriptive of the fort itself as being 'Strong as Lugh'.

Then there is the Lugudunum or 'Hillfort of Lugh' of the Ravenna Cosmography. This place, according to Rivet and Smith's *The Place-Names of Roman Britain*, is situated somewhere roughly between Chester-le-Street and South Shields. The only good candidate would seem to be Penshaw Hill, which the Brigantes Nation website calls "the only triple rampart Iron Age hillfort known to exist in the north of England." Penshaw Hill is associated with the famous Lambton Worm, a monster not unlike the two worms or dragons of Lleu's hillfort of Dinas Emrys in Gwynedd, Wales.

Yet another Lugh's Fort is found at Dreva Craig near Merlin's Drumelzier, and I will have cause to discuss this site in more detail below.

According to Joseph Rogerson (*The Farmer's Magazine*, 1835), the Melrose Lammas Fair (Christian substitute for the Pagan Lughnasadh) was the largest in the south of Scotland. It was held on the northern slope of the Eildons, and as many as 30,000–50,000 lambs were shown. Lammas was associated with St. Peter 'in Chains' – i.e., St. Peter when he was imprisoned by Herod. His being freed by an angel, according to James B. Jordan (*The Resurrection of Peter and the Coming of the Kingdom*, Biblical Horizons, 34), portrayed a type of resurrection for Peter, recapitulating the resurrection of Jesus. As I've shown that the death of Lugh fell on Imbolc (February 1st – see below) on the opposite side of the solar year from Lughnasadh, we can say with a fair degree of confidence that not only were the Eildons a famous Lugh mountain, but that the celebration of Lughnasadh here had commemorated the rebirth of the sun god.

The Eildons are noted for the stories of 'Canonbie' or Canonbie Dick and Thomas the Rhymer of Ercildoune.

Canonbie is close to both the Carwinley of Myrddin's/Merlin's lord Gwenddolau, and Arthuret Knowes – the scene of the Battle of Arfderydd in which Myrddin was driven mad. The thirteenth-century Thomas is credited with meeting an elf-woman under the Eildon Tree (the location of which is now marked by a stone) and being taken under the Eildons to the Land of Faery. He is also credited with a prophecy concerning Merlin's grave at Drumelzier:

> "When Tweed and Powsail meet at Merlin's grave, Scotland and England that day a king shall have."

The story of Canonbie Dick presents Thomas as a wizard from past days, and I will quote it in full:

> "A long time ago in the Borders Region there lived a horse cowper called Canonbie Dick. He was both admired and feared for his bold courage and rash temper. One evening, he was riding over Bowden Moor on the west side of the Eildon Hills. It was very late, and the moon was already high in the night sky.
>
> He had been to market, but trade that day had been poor, and he had with him a brace of horses, which he had not been able to sell. Suddenly, he saw ahead of him on the moonlit road a stranger. The stranger was dressed in a fashion that had not been seen for many centuries. The stranger politely asked the price of the horses.
>
> Now Canonbie Dick liked to bargain, and was not worried by the strange man's looks. Why, he would have sold his horses to the Devil himself and cheated him as well, given half a chance. They agreed on a price which the stranger promptly paid.
>
> The only puzzle was that the gold coins he used to pay were as ancient as his dress. They were in the shape of unicorns and bonnet pieces. However, Canonbie Dick shrugged his shoulders. Gold was gold. He smiled to himself, thinking that he would get a better bargain for the coins than the stranger had got for the horses.

When the stranger asked if he could meet him again at the same place, Canonbie Dick was happy to agree. But the stranger had one condition: that he should always come by night and always alone.

After several more meetings, Canonbie Dick became curious to learn more about his secret buyer. He suggested that 'dry bargains' were unlucky bargains and that they should seal the business with a drink at the buyer's home.

'You may see my dwelling if you wish,' said the stranger, 'but if you lose courage at what you see there, you will regret it all your life.'

Canonbie Dick was scornful of the warning. After all, he was well-known for his courage, and the stranger seemed harmless enough. The stranger led the way along a narrow footpath, which led into the hills between the southern and central peaks to a place called the Lucken Hare. Canonbie Dick followed but was amazed to see an enormous entrance into the hillside. He knew the area well but had never seen before such an opening or heard any mention of it.

They dismounted and tethered their horses. His guide stopped and fixed his gaze on Canonbie Dick. 'You may still return,' he said. Not wanting to be seen as a coward, Canonbie Dick shook his head, squared his shoulders and followed the man along the passage into a great hall cut out of the rock.

As they walked, they passed many rows of stables. In every stall there was a coal-black horse, and by every horse lay a knight in jet-black armour, with a drawn sword in each hand. They were as still as stone, as if they had been carved from marble.

In the great hall were many burning torches, but their fiery light only made the hall gloomier. There was a strange stillness in the air, like a hot day before a storm. At last, they arrived at the far end of the hall. On an antique oak table lay a sword, still sheathed, and a horn. The stranger revealed that he was Thomas of Ercildoun [Thomas the Rhymer], the famous prophet who had disappeared many centuries ago.

Turning to Canonbie Dick, he said, 'It is foretold that: *He that sounds the horn and draws that sword shall, if his heart fails him not, be king over all broad Britain. But all depends on courage, and whether the sword or horn is taken first. So speaks the tongue that cannot lie.*'

The stillness of the air felt heavy. Canonbie Dick wanted to take the sword, but he was struck by a supernatural terror such as he had never felt before. What, he thought, would happen if he drew the sword? Would such a daring act annoy the powers of the mountain?

Instead, he took the horn and with trembling hands put it to his lips. He let out a feeble blast that echoed around the hall.

It produced a terrible answer. Thunder rolled, and with a cry and a clash of armour, the knights arose from their slumber, and the horses snorted and tossed their manes. A dreadful army rose before him. Terrified, Canonbie Dick snatched the sword and tried to free it from its scabbard. At this, a voice boomed:

'Woe to the Coward, that ever he was born,

Who did not draw the sword before he blew the horn.'

Then he heard the fury of a great whirlwind as he was lifted from his feet and blasted from the cavern. He tumbled down steep banks of stones until he hit the ground. Canobie Dick was found the next morning by local shepherds. He had just enough trembling breath to tell his fearful tale, before he died."

A similar story is told of Alderley Edge in Cheshire, but in that version the wizard is Merlin and the sleeping knights are King Arthur and his men. My guess is that in the case of the Canonbie

Dick story, Thomas the Rhymer has taken the place of Merlin. This is not a new supposition, but combined with my identification of Myrddin's Noquetran with Eildon Mid Hill as the Dolorous Mountain, the argument is significantly strengthened. Fergus was written around 1200 CE, while Thomas is thought to have lived c.1220–1298. At some point, Thomas appears to have been substituted for Merlin at his chapel/cairn on Eildon Mid Hill.

If I am right and the Eildons are Merlin's Mountain at the centre of the great Celyddon Wood, then we can allow for the Celyddon as being thought of as the ancient woodland which covered much of the area surrounding the Eildons. When we combine this with the fact that Merlin was obviously wandering in the wood in the vicinity of Drumelzier when he was captured by Meldred, then it is fairly obvious that the Celyddon (which, in this context, means merely a great forest of the Scottish Lowlands) extended for a considerable distance.

Indeed, we know there were four great ancient forests surrounding the Eildon Hills: the Jedforest, whose Capon Tree oak is one of the oldest such trees in all of Britain; Teviotdale itself, which was covered by huge oaks and ash trees in the twelfth century; the Ettrick Forest of Selkirkshire; and the Lauder Forest, an immense forested tract encompassing Lauderdale that still existed up until the seventeenth century. Apples, or rather crab-apples, the very species of tree Merlin takes refuge under in the early Welsh poetry, were also present in this region. The St. Boswell's Apple is thought to be 150 years old and is the largest of its kind in Scotland. Thomas the Rhymer, taken to Fairyland at the Eildons, is given an apple by the Queen of Fairy.

In my book, *The Arthur of History*, I was able to precisely pinpoint the location of Arthur's Coed Celyddon battle. This was in the area of the Caddon Water, a place-name with early forms (spellings) that are all but identical to that of Celyddon. The Caddon Water empties into the Tweed not far west of the Eildons. In fact, it was likely this stream name that led to the relocation of Caledonia from its home in the Scottish Highlands to the Lowlands in Welsh tradition.

THE PRE-ROMANCE MOUNTAIN OF MYRDDIN

While the Eildons would seem to be the location of Merlin's Mountain according to the late 'Fergus' romance, there is evidence of another Scottish Lowland mountain in the earlier Welsh poetry. This particular mountain may have been the true, original mountain, the prototype of all those that succeeded it. Or it may simply have been another of several mountains sacred to Lleu.

The reference to the location of this mountain is found in *Gwasgargerd vyrdin yny bed* – the *Separation-Song of Myrddin in the Grave* of *The Red Book of Hergest*. There, Myrddin says:

> 'Gwasawg, your cry to Gwenddydd
> was told to me by the wild men of the mountain
> in Aber Caraf.'

From other references in the early poetry, we know that Gwasawg was a 'supporter' of the Christian champion Rhydderch Hael, King of Strathclyde. The name is a diminutive of Welsh *gwas* – 'lad, servant'.

As it turns out, St. Kentigern as a boy (see Chapter 8 of Jocelyn's *Vita*) is called servuli, from servulus, a dim. of Latin servus, with a meaning of 'servant-lad, young slave'.

As Kentigern is brought into close connection with Myrddin as Lailoken in the saint's life, and Kentigern's royal patron was Rhydderch, I'm proposing that Gwasawg is a Welsh rendering of servuli, and that the former is thus St. Kentigern himself.

Note that Myrddin is said to be chased by the hunting-dogs of Rhydderch, and Kentigern or *Cuno-tigernos means 'Hound Lord'.

While Aber Caraf has been rendered by at least one translator as Aber Craf (Peter Goodrich, *The Romance of Merlin*, 1990), a location in south-central Wales, we can be sure it is actually to be found in Lowland Scotland.

We have seen how Merlin/Lailoken is present in both the region of Glasgow and at Drumelzier on the Tweed. It has long been thought that his mountain must have been somewhere between these two places, and most likely at or not far from the sources of the Clyde and Tweed, a sort of symbolic 'centre' of the southern 'Caledonian Wood'.

I would identify the mountain in Aber Caraf with Tinto Hill (2320 feet / 707 meters), which looms over ancient Abercarf, now called Wiston. Abercarf, according to the Scottish Place-Name Society's *Brittonic Language in the Old North*, is from *aber*, 'confluence', plus *garw*, 'rough', derived from the name of the Garf Water, a tributary of the upper Clyde. I also call attention to Wyndales on the mountain's flank, a name which, superficially at least, reminds us of the Gwenddolau or White Dales of Carwinley near Arthuret/Arderydd.

When I asked Alan James, the author of *BLITON*, as to the possibility that Abercarf could instead contain *carw*, 'stag', he responded:

> "Quite right. As to the merits of the two interpretations, I'm agnostic. The phonology of either wouldn't be difficult to explain. *Garw* and Gaelic *garbh* are, of course, pretty common in river-names, and I'm rather less eager than some place-name scholars to see animals, e.g. *carw*, in such names, but there certainly are parallels."

Just a few kilometers upstream on the Clyde from the Garf Water is Hartside and Hartside Burn. Red deer were once plentiful here.

Given Myrddin's association with the stag in Geoffrey of Monmouth's *Life of Merlin* – and his placement historically at Arfderydd/Arderydd/Arthuret in Cumbria, in what was the north-western limit of the ancient Carvetti (Stag-people) territory – a mountain at the confluence of the 'Stag Water' would make a lot of sense.

Tinto Hill is situated between Drumelzier to the east and Glasgow to the northwest. It is also only a few miles north-northwest of the headwaters of the Clyde and Tweed. Thus, it just happens to stand exactly where we would expect the hill of Myrddin to be found.

The hill's name was discussed long ago by W.J. Watson in his *General Survey of Ayrshire and Strathclyde – History of the Celtic Place-names of Scotland*, 1926 (reprinted 1993 by BIRLINN, Edinburgh, ISBN 1874744068):

> "Tinto appears in 'Karyn de Tintou', 'Kaerne de Tintou', c.1315 (RMS); in Macfarlane it is Tyntoche once, Tynto thrice; in Scots, Tintock, as also in the *Retours*; it is for teinteach, 'place of fire'…"

Atop Tinto Hill is Tinto Cairn. It is of Bronze Age date and the largest summit cairn in all of Scotland. Details on the hill and cairn can be found here:

> http://canmore.rcahms.gov.uk/en/site/47525/details/tinto+cairn/
> http://www.undiscoveredscotland.co.uk/biggar/tinto/index.html
> http://www.scotlandsplaces.gov.uk/search_item/image.php?service=RCAHMS&id=47525&image_id=SC342977

Different reasons have been supplied for why this hill is called 'place of fire'. One suggests it gets its name from the fact that its exposed red felsite rock can be given a fiery glow by the setting sun.

Another possible explanation is that the hill was used for beacon fires or even for Beltane fires:

"Long a beacon post and a place of Beltane fires, it took thence its name of Tinto, signifying the 'hill of fire'" (Groome, 1885, *Ordnance Gazetteer of Scotland*).

I would say that these apparently conflicting ideas are not mutually exclusive. Indeed, it may precisely have been the red glowing colour of the rocks in the light of the setting sun that drew people to this mountain as being particularly sacred, and they may then have used it for Beltane fires.

It would surely be significant if Myrddin were thought to be communing with the ancestral ghosts at a huge Bronze Age cairn atop a mountain known as the Place of Fire. This would intimately connect him with seasonal Beltane rites.

THE APPLE TREE OF MYRDDIN

In the early Welsh poem *Yr Afallennau*, 'The Apple Trees', we are told about a magical apple tree in which Myrddin the Mad finds refuge from the British Strathclyde king, Rhydderch. We are given various enigmatic hints as to the location of this tree. The tree is in the Celyddon Wood (in this case, the Scottish Lowland forest deriving its name from the Caddon Water, a relocation of the true Caledonian Forest that lay in the Highlands). It is said to be "beyond Rhun", and in a glade (Awallen peren atif inllanerch). Also, it is on a bank of a river.

Many have dispensed with this tree as a mythological construct. I once tried to identify it with Cairn Avel (from W. *afal*, 'apple'?), a chambered tomb in Dumfries and Galloway. However, certain antiquarian writers did point out that the Welsh common noun *llanerch* or 'glade' was present in the Scottish Lowland place-name Lanark. The *Geiriadur Prifysgol Cymru* has for the entry on llanerch:

"llanerch
[?llan+erch1 neu ynteu est. yn -rk- i'r Frth. *landa (> llann),
H. Grn. lanherch, gl. saltus; digwydd mewn e. lleoedd yng
Nghumbria ac yn yr Alban, e.e. Lanercost, Lanark, Lanrick,
Lendrick, Caerlanrig]
eb.g. (bach. g. llanerchyn) ll. llanerchau, -i, -oedd, -ydd,
llanneirch, llenneirch, llennyrch.
Lle agored mewn coedwig, &c., gwerddon, tir porfa, cowrt,
beili, man gwag, clwt, mangre, lle, ardal; brycheuyn,
ysmotyn; (geir.) trigfa; Her. maes neu wyneb tarian:
a clearing, glade, oasis, pasture, court, empty space, patch,
place, area, region; blemish, spot; (dict.) habitation; field of
escutcheon (in her.)."

Alas, no one seems to have paid attention to this observation. Yet the connection has been confirmed by the best of the modern place-name scholars. The following is from Alan G. James' *The Brittonic Language in the Old North: A Guide to the Place-Name Evidence, Volume 2, Guide to the Elements*:

"lanerc or *lanrec (f) Br *landā- (see lann) + -arcā- > OW(LL) lannerch > M-MnW llannerch. The suffix -arcā- may be diminutive, cf. early Modern Welsh glosses llan = Latin area, llannerch = areola (see GPC, and Williams 1952). If so, and assuming a secular sense for lann (which see), the meaning would be 'a small (cleared, and possibly enclosed) area of (former) scrub, waste, fallow or wooded land.' The common interpretation 'a glade' may overemphasise the woodland connotations. The examples from the north mostly show single –n- and non-spirant –rc. Jackson (1955a), at p164, regarded the latter as a Pritenic feature, but it was probably also present in northernmost Brittonic.

The cluster of names with this element in and around the middle Irthing valley, recorded mainly in the *Lanercost Cartulary* (Todd, 1997), is of particular interest. Jackson argued, in *LHEB* §149, pp.571-2, that the absence of spirant lenition from these names may indicate that [-rk] > [-rχ], which he dated to the late sixth century in west Brittonic, occurred later or not at all in northern Brittonic/Cumbric (assuming, as he did, that these names were adopted by Northumbrian English-speakers on their arrival, again in the late sixth century). However, this begs several questions, and his later opinion on the similar feature in Pritenic (1955a loc. cit.) suggests an alternative view that these names may reflect much later colonisation of the district by settlers from further north (though not necessarily from Pictland): see A.G. James (2008) at p200.

Several forms also show metathesised –rec, which may be compared with Landrick Per (x2) and Lendrick Ang and Knr. R.A.V. Cox (1997) shows that such metathesis was characteristic of Gaelicised forms of this word. This may be relevant to the names north of the Forth, and even to the local pronunciation of Lanark recorded as Lainrick. However, it is doubtful whether the names in the *Lanercost Cartulary* are Gaelic or Goidelic-influenced.

'Rhun', if considered in the context of Rhydderch's Strathclyde, can only be a reference to the ninth-century Strathclyde king of that name. Now, critics have claimed that Rhun's kingdom could not be that which appears in the Myrddin poem. Why? Because Myrddin was of the sixth century. But these same critics forget that *Yr Afallennau* is extant only in MSS. dated well after the reign of Rhun. So by the time the poem was put to paper – regardless of any prior verbal transmission – the kingdom of Strathclyde might easily have been anachronistically called the Land of Rhun in the medieval Welsh poem.

I thought to begin my search by looking for an actual apple tree place-name in the vicinity of Lanark. The result of that search?

There was a chapel associated with nearby Nemphlar called variously 'All Men's Apple Tree' or 'Old Man's Apple Tree'. Some rather dated books discuss this place, but the best information is to be found on more modern and very respectable websites:

http://www.wosas.net/wosas_site.php?id=10265
https://canmore.org.uk/site/46641/nemphlar-church

The location of the chapel is shown only on the Roy maps of 1752-55. It is near the Clyde, the chief river of the Kingdom of Strathclyde. I take this to be the river mentioned in the *Yr Afallennau*.

Alan James, a foremost expert in the Brittonic place-names of North Britain, has informed me that:

"Very helpful friends in the FB Scottish Place-Names group have come up with more on Nemphlar. The earliest record is a grant 1173x1214 by King William to the parish church of Lanark of the parish of Nemflare (sic in the rubric, in the text of the grant, Nenflare).

There is no record of any Templar holding there, notwithstanding Chalmers (who gives no source), Alan Macquarrie has confirmed that."

I would hasten to add that very near where this apple tree chapel was said to have stood, there was a holy well. It went by various names, but came to be associated with St. Mary:

https://canmore.org.uk/site/46640/nemphlar-my-ladys-well

Why might this be important? Because in Strophe 4 of *Yr Afallennau* we are told that Myrddin "contended at its base [of the apple tree], in order to please a maiden." As the chapel of the apple tree and the holy well were very close to one another, it may be that the maiden in question was the Pagan equivalent of the Virgin Mary.

Lanark is the only place in Scotland to have an actual ancient church dedicated to St. Kentigern. Other churches are always dedicated to his nickname, Mungo.

> https://saintsplaces.gla.ac.uk/place.php?id=1335890004

Kentigern is elsewhere brought into connection with Merlin/Myrddin, and I have convincingly shown that this saint appears in the Welsh Myrddin poems as a certain Gwasawg (see http://mistshadows.blogspot.com/2017/07/slight-revision-of-merlinmyrddin.html). Gwasawg is the "supporter of Rhydderch" and thus an enemy of Myrddin, and is mentioned in the *Yr Afallennau*.

This chapel of the apple tree is only some 15km as the crow flies from Myrddin's Tinto Hill (see http://mistshadows.blogspot.com/2018/02/ive-been-asked-to-post-my-study-on.html). Tinto is the 'central mountain' of the Scottish Lowlands, at least in the scheme presented to us in the early Myrddin tradition.

Lastly, it would appear that the Nemphlar region was quite famous for its apples.

> "Blaeu's map of the Upper and Nether Wards of Clydesdale, based on Pont's 1596 survey, shows a figure holding a basket of apples, a reference to the prosperous orchards of the Clyde Valley."

Given all of the above, I would put forward the proposal that Myrddin's apple tree in the Celyddon Wood of Lowland Scotland is none other than the All Men's Apple Tree/Old Man's Apple Tree chapel of Nemphlar in South Lanarkshire.

NOTE: Alan James has shared with me a possibly interesting derivation for the All Men's portion of the apple tree name:

"According to *OPS* (p119), Nemphlar, in the reign of King William the Lion (reign 1165–1214), seems to have had a church of its own, which, after its annexation by that king to Lanark, became a chapel dependent on the mother church. Its site was at East Nemphlar, probably at a spot called 'Alman's appletree'. Roy's 1755 map records this spot as Allman's Appletree, located near NS859446, where My Lady's Well is now mapped.

The Nemphlar apple tree seems to be first recorded on Roy's map, at a time when apple cultivation was only starting to get going, and in enclosed gardens and orchards, so this would have been either a notable crab apple tree or, less likely, an even more exceptional planted one.

Simon Taylor notes: 1173x1214 the whole parish of Nemphlar and Cartlan was granted by King William to church of Lanark, and thereafter remained a pendicle of that church, which itself was annexed to Dryburgh Abbey (Dryburgh Lib. nos. 44–6; Retours nos. 325, 328). Cowan 1967, pp.154–5.

My (AJ) immediate thoughts: those are helpful, if only in confirming a fair degree of consistency over eight centuries or so - /n/ > /m/ is the only real phonemic-level change, and that's unsurprising before /f/.

Alman's Appletree is tantalising, it might just possibly have been a meeting-place (ON al-manna)."

THE NAME MYRDDIN

According to Dr. Graham Isaac of The National University of Ireland, Galway, the name Myrddin may be from an earlier, not directly attested *Myr-ddyn, with the second element *dyn* 'man, person', and the first element *Myr-* which is found in the name of the Old Irish goddess-type figure Morrigan (who also prophesizes), in English night-mare, and also in several Slavic words. This original form would have been something like *morodonyes, 'man-demon, spectre' or 'man of supernatural character' (see Isaac, G., 2001, *Myrddin, proffwyd diwedd y byd: ystyriaethau newydd ar ddatblygiad ei chwedl*, Llên Cymru, 24:13-23).

Thus, the basic meaning of the name Myrddin was 'supernatural being, elf, goblin, phantom', or the like. Another possible rendering would be something like 'Elf-man'. His father's name was Morfryn or Mor-bryn; according to Isaac, literally 'Elf-hill'.

I myself prefer Isaac's derivation for Myrddin's name, and I will have more to say on why I do so below.

Myrddin may also reflect a Welsh attempt to render a Gaelic name meaning 'mad-man', itself either dependent on or at the root of the homo fatuus designation for Llallogan found in the *Life of St. Kentigern*. According to Dr. Simon Rodway of The University of Wales, if an Irish compound *merduine* ('mad person') existed, it could be 'semi-translated' into Welsh as *Myrddyn*, becoming Myrddin in the same way as that envisaged by Isaac. *The Electronic Dictionary of the Irish Language* does not give any examples of *merduine*, but it is not implausible as a compound in the light of *mergall* 'mad foreigner', *merscal* 'mad phantom', etc. Professor Ranko Matasovic can "imagine an OIr. compound *mer-duine* 'crazy man' somehow calqued or partly borrowed into Welsh."

These etymologies have been put forward against the traditional one, i.e. that Myrddin is a very straight-forward rendering of Moridunum, the 'Sea-fort'. Geoffrey of Monmouth, in fact, claimed that Myrddin is to be derived from the city-name of Carmarthen, ancient Caerfyrddin, Roman Moridunum, 'Sea-fort'. In *The History of the Kings of Britain*, Myrddin is found as a boy at Carmarthen. The whole story is Geoffrey's alteration of Nennius' tale of the boy Ambrosius being found at Campus Elleti in Glamorgan.

The only father provided for Myrddin in the early poetry is one Morfryn. I think this name, despite what Isaac has to say about it, rather transparently means 'Sea-hill' and is probably a literally creation, as the -dunum of Moridunum originally had the sense of 'hillfort'. Native forts were typically built atop hills.

Myrddin's brothers were named Morgenau, Morial, Mordaf and Morien. According to A.O.H. Jarmon, Morien is 'Sea-born', but the rest contain Mor-, *mawr*, 'great'. They may all, however, "reflect an early association, perhaps mythological, with the sea." John Koch, in *The Celtic Lands* (in *Medieval Arthurian Literature: A Guide to Recent Sources*), says that:

> "References in the Cyfoesi to Myrddin's father, Morfryn, and brothers, Morgenau, Morial, Mordaf and Morien, imply that, when the tradition was formed, the name [Myrddin] was still understood to contain the element *mor* < *mori-*, 'sea'."

A 'Sea-man' makes no sense, as there is nothing of the merman about Myrddin! The sea does not figure in his story at all. Some have sought to use 'Sea-man' as a way to link Myrddin with Mannanan mac Lir of Irish story. But, again, there is nothing of Mannanan in Myrddin.

Other attempted etymologies for the name Myrddin fail on either phonological or philological bases, or both.

THE NAME LLALLOG/LLALLOGAN

Myrddin in the early poems is called Llallog or Llallogan, a name also found in *The Life of St. Kentigern* as 'Laloecen'. This is a reduplicated form of *ail/eil*, 'other', and so Llallogan is, literally, 'The Other' or, perhaps, 'The One from the Other[world]'.

Llallog is present in feminine form in the name of Patrick's sister's daughter Lalloc, who was set over Ard Senlis in Ireland.

This place was on Magh-Nenda, where the famous fairy hill Sidh-Nenta was also to be found. The modern name for Senlis is Fairymount. St. Lalloc of the Fairymount would then seem to represent 'the Other' who was the fairy queen or divine ancestral spirit of this particular sidh-dwelling.

We also know of a ninth-century Breton named Lalocan, mentioned in the *Cartulaire de l'Abbaye de Redon* (125).

Welsh Ellyll, cognate with the Irish personal name Ailill, is also a reduplicated form of *ail/eil*, 'other'. Ellyll, according to the *Geiriadur Prufysgol Cymru*, is defined as: "goblin, elf, fairy, sprit, genius (of a place), apparition, phantom, spectre, wraith, ghost, shade, bogey."

To quote from Professor Daniel Melia of the University of California, Berkeley (personal communication):

"I'm citing *CELTICA3*, 1956, which reads as follows:

'The contracted form of Ailill gen. Ailella in all the manuscripts of the genealogies which I have read (Rawl. B 502; Laud 610; LL; BB; Lec.; H 2.7) is always Aill-, Aill-a. These contractions are quite abnormal.

Ailill is without a doubt cognate with Welsh *ellyll* 'ghost, elf, etc.', and this suggests that the older form of the name was Aillill which became Ailill with the same kind of dissimilation we find in *cenand < cenn-fhind* and *menand < menn-fhind*.

The *Geiriadur Prifysgol Cymru* agrees with this meaning. They see a connection with a reduplicated form of Proto-Celtic **allo-* 'other' as in the Gaulish tribal name 'Allobroges' < **allo* 'other' + *bro-* 'border' -> 'country'. The Wurzburg glosses on the Pauline Epistles (Wb.) date from ~600 – ~750, so the form 'Aillill' would presumably, by O'Brien's argument, have still been current, at least amongst literate intellectuals, in that period."

Professor Ranko Matasovic of *The Etymological Lexicon of Proto-Celtic* (again, via private correspondence) says:

> "Welsh *ellyll* is indeed cognate with Mir. Ailill, but these names cannot be related to English 'elf', which is from Germanic **albiyo-*. It is certainly possible that these words contain the stem **al-* (actually **h2el-*, in a more modern notation), the plain pronominal stem that meant 'other, different' (Lat. alius, Gr. allos, etc.). I would add that Alladhan, the name given to Llallogan in the Irish *Suibhne Geilt* story, would appear to be from Irish *allaid*, 'wild'. The most likely etymology for *allaid* is the same *al-* root, as an 'Other' is someone who lived beyond the civilized world and was hence barbarous or 'wild', a stranger or foreigner or an enemy – i.e., someone deemed dangerous because he did not belong to one's native land. The evolution of meaning would be similar to the development from Latin silvaticus, 'belonging to woods' to French sauvage."

Dr. Graham Isaac of The National University of Ireland, Galway, and Professor of Celtic, Thomas Charles-Edwards of Jesus College, Oxford, both agree with this derivation for *ellyll*/Ailill.

I would add that Rachel Bromwich, in her note to *Welsh Triad No. 63*, says of the word *ellyll* in the context of three heroes:

> "... the suggested implication of *ellyll* is that of men who became 'outside' themselves."

This is significant, given that one of these three heroes – Llyr Marini – is, in late genealogies, placed in the tribe of Meirchiaun. I've shown that Meirchiaun ruled from the heartland of the Carvetii or Stag-People. A variant of *Triad 63* calls Llyr a *"charv/charw ellyll"* or 'stag-spectre'.

There is one more possible application of the name Llallogan, this time to an entity who may be a real god on Hadrian's Wall.

I'm referring, of course, to Alletios at Corbridge. My discussion of this deity may be found at https://mistshadows.blogspot.com/2019/04/camelot-at-corbridge-god-allitio-and.html.

In the Irish, the use of a word for 'phantom' is applied to the god Lugh. The following selection is from *Baile in Scail*, 'The Phantom's Frenzy':

> "They saw the scál [phantom] himself in the house, before them on his throne. There was never in Tara a man of his size or his beauty, on account of the fairness of his form and the wondrousness of his appearance.

He answered them and said, 'I am not a phantom nor a spectre. I have come on account of my fame among you, since my death. And I am of the race of Adam: my name is Lugh son of Eithliu son of Tigernmas. This is why I have come: to relate to you the length of your reign, and of every reign which there will be in Tara.'

And the girl who sat before then in the house was the Sovereignty of Ireland, and it was she who gave Conn his meal: the rib of an ox and the rib of a boar. The ox rib was twenty-four feet long and eight feet between its arch and the ground. When the girl began to distribute drinks she said, 'To whom shall this cup be given?' – and the phantom answered her.

When she had named every ruler until the Day of Judgment, they went into the phantom's shadow, so that they saw neither the enclosure nor the house. The vat and the golden dipper and the cup were left with Conn. And hence are the stories *The Phantom's Dream* and *The Adventure and Journey of Conn*.

The primary sense was 'a ghost, a supernatural being', especially a powerful one – but in Welsh, Irish and Scottish Gaelic literatures, it is used of human heroes – and in Welsh it comes to mean 'a young warrior'.

An Irish '*ferscal*', then, comes very close to Myrddin/Llallogan in meaning.

THE CELYDDON WOOD AS THE LAND OF SPIRITS

The ancient Classical writer Procopius (in his sixth-century CE *History of the Wars*, VIII, XX. 42–48) said:

> "Now in this island of Britain the men of ancient times built a long wall, cutting off a large part of it; and the climate and the soil and everything else is not alike on the two sides of it. For to the south of the wall there is a salubrious air, changing with the seasons, being moderately warm in summer and cool in winter … But on the north side, everything is the reverse of this, so that it is actually impossible for a man to survive there even a half-hour, but countless snakes and serpents and every other kind of wild creature occupy this area as their own. And, strangest of all, the inhabitants say that if a man crosses this wall and goes to the other side, he dies straightaway … They say, then, that the souls of men who die are always conveyed to this place."

From the Welsh poem *The Dialogue of Myrddin and Taliesin* (in *The Black Book of Carmarthen*), we learn that at Myrddin's Battle of Arderydd:

> "Seven score chieftains became gwyllon; in the Wood of Celyddon they died."

Gwyllon or 'Wild Ones' is a word deriving from *gwyllt*, 'wild'. The Welsh epithet for Myrddin is, of course, Gwyllt. Myrddin Gwyllt is Myrddin 'the Wild'.

But as Nikolai Tolstoy pointed out, there is something odd about these two lines. The gwyllon or 'Wild Ones' are equated with the warriors who died in the battle! The word 'died' in the poem's second line is Middle Welsh *daruuan*, i.e. *darfuan*. Modern Welsh has *darfyddaf* or *darfod* which, according to the authoritative *Geiriadur Prifysgol Cymru* Welsh dictionary, has the following meanings:

> "To come to an end, end, conclude, finish, complete, terminate, cease; expire, die, languish, weaken, fail, fade, decline, perish."

Darfod is an interesting word. It is from the prefix *dar-*, roughly 'across', and *bod*, 'to be', with the regular lenition of *b>f*. So literally 'to be across', possibly in the same sense in which we say of a dead person, 'he has crossed over'.

There is thus no ambiguity in the poetic passage we are considering. The warriors who became 'Wild Ones' did not go mad – they died. In this context, then, to become gwyllon means to become a roving spirit that has left its battle-slain body behind. To exist as a 'Wild One' is to exist in spirit-form after the death of the body.

The Christian medieval mind either could not accept this notion of wandering spirits or, just as likely, misunderstood it. The gwyllon were transformed into living madmen who leapt or flitted about the forest much as did their Irish counterpart, Suibhne Geilt, or the British madman Fer Caille/Alladhan, mentioned in the story of Suihbne.

In another Myrddin poem, *Greetings* (in *The Black Book of Carmarthen*), we are told by Myrddin himself that:

> "The hwimleian speaks to me strange tidings, and I prophesy a summer of strife."

Hwimleian or 'Grey Wanderer' is yet another word for a spirit or spectre.

We might then naturally conclude that Myrddin's madness was of the same kind – i.e., he had died at the Battle of Arderydd. The triple sacrifice he suffers at Drumelzier at the hands of Meldred's shepherds would then be a 'tag on', made necessary because his already having died was no longer acknowledged and because it was politic to give him a Christian burial. I will, in fact, later show that the Drumelzier tradition is a relocalized one, and that Myrddin does not really belong there at all. However, the fact that his triple-death at Drumelzier is a sacred one, and one that mimics the death of the god Lleu in Welsh tradition, is significant. The death is SACRIFICIAL in nature, and such triple deaths were meted out to HUMAN sacrifice victims (see Ross and Robins' *The Life and Death of a Druid Prince*).

Among the ancient Celts and Germans, we have some testimony from Classical authors that war captives were the most commonly sacrificed humans. It is not impossible that Myrddin was captured after the disastrous defeat at Arderydd and sacrificed by his enemy, although since that enemy seems to have been the Christian king Rhydderch, this is a difficult proposition to support. Perhaps a Pagan ally of Rhydderch got his hands on Llallogan. Or Llallogan had fled to a neighbouring tribal territory and was seized by an opportunistic chieftain.

Even more likely is that Myrddin was offered up to Lleu to ensure victory in the upcoming contest with Rhydderch. It is Ross and Robins' belief that the Lindow Man was sacrificed by his own people to ensure victory over the Romans. If this is what really happened, then his death and spiritual flight at the Arderydd battle may have been a misreading of his being ritually slain on the eve of the said battle.

In the Irish sources, we are told of 'battle-panic' and one of its unfortunate results. For example, when the great hero Cuchulainn faces the opposing armies of Ireland, "He saw from him the ardent sparkling of the bright golden weapons over the heads of the four great provinces of Eriu, before the fall of the cloud of evening. Great fury and indignation seized him on seeing them, at the number of his opponents and at the multitude of his enemies. He seized his two spears, and his shield and his sword, and uttered from his throat a warrior's shout, so that sprites, and satyrs, and maniacs of the valley, and the demons of the air responded, terror-stricken by the shout which he had raised on high. And the Neman confused the army; and the four provinces of Eriu dashed themselves against the points of their own spears and weapons, so that one hundred warriors died of fear and trembling in the middle of the fort and encampment that night."

This passage is from W.M. Hennessey's *The Ancient Irish Goddess of War*. Also, from this source:

"Of the effects of this fear inspired by the Badb [or Nemhain] was *geltacht* or lunacy, which, according to the popular notion, affected the body no less than the mind, and, in fact, made its victims so that they flew through the air like birds."

We learn more about the precise meaning of *geltacht* from *The Electronic Dictionary of the Irish Language*. There, we are told:

"*geltacht* –
Keywords: panic; terror; frenzy; insanity."

In Thomas Kinsella's translation of *The Tain*, we learn that:

"The Nemain brought confusion on the armies and a hundred of their number [while asleep!] fell dead."

"... that same night, Net's wives, Nemain and Badb, called out to the men of Ireland near the field of Gairech and Irgairech, and a hundred warriors died of fright."

In *The Saintly Madman: A Study of the Scholarly Reception History of Buile Shuibhne* by Alexandra Bergholm, Department of Comparative Religion, University of Helsinki (2009), we are given a wonderful description of what happened to the title character when he was faced with the horror of battle:

"When the Battle of Mag Rath begins, Suibhne is suddenly alarmed by the cries of the two hosts, and the incident is depicted as follows:

> ... he looked up, whereupon turbulence [?], and darkness, and fury, and giddiness, and frenzy, and flight, unsteadiness, restlessness, and unquiet filled him; likewise disgust with every place in which he used to be and desire for every place which he had not reached. His fingers were palsied, his feet trembled, his heart beat quick, his senses were overcome, his sight was distorted, his weapons fell naked from his hands, so that through Ronan's curse he went, like any bird of the air, in madness and imbecility."

It should be noted here immediately that the word translated as 'fury' is nemhain – the goddess's name used as a common noun.

When we come to the two accounts of the Battle of Arderydd, we see that *The Life of St. Kentigern* preserves the more authentic tradition (although highly Christianized, of course), while that found in Geoffrey of Monmouth's *Life of Merlin* is considerably diluted:

St. Kentigern's Life –

> "In the midst of that fray, the very sky began to gape open above my head, and I heard what seemed to be a great cracking sound, a voice in the sky saying to me, 'Lailoken, Lailoken, since you alone are guilty of the blood of all your slain comrades, you alone shall suffer for their sins. You shall be handed over to the minions of Satan, and until the day of your death your companions shall be the beasts of the forest.' And, as I turned my eyes to the source of the voice, I saw a brilliance so dazzling that no man could bear it. I also saw numerous battle formations of an army in the

sky, much like the streaks of lightning. In their hands, the warriors held burning lances and shining javelins which they brandished at me with bloodthirsty FURY [emphasis mine]. Then, as I turned away, a wicked spirit seized me and consigned me to live among the wild beasts of the forest, as you are my witness."

Life of Merlin –

"Then, when the air was full of these repeated loud complainings [of Merlin's grief], a strange madness came upon him. He crept away and fled to the woods, unwilling that any should see his going. Into the forest he went; glad to lie hidden beneath the ash trees. He watched the wild creatures grazing on the pasture of the glades. Sometimes he would follow them, sometimes pass them in his course. He made use of the roots of plants and of grasses, of fruit from the trees, and of the blackberries of the thicket. He became a Man of the Woods ['silvester homo' – the Fer Caille title given to him in the story of Suibhne Geilt], as if dedicated to the woods. So, for a whole summer he stayed hidden in the woods, discovered by none, forgetful of himself and of his own, lurking like a wild thing."

The author Hennessey, like the Christian medieval audience of the Merlin story, did not realize that madness could be a poetic metaphor for a spectral death-state, sometimes brought about through unbearable fear. It was not the demented body that fled like a bird through the forest after a battle – something physically impossible – but the spirit of the warrior whose death was literally caused by the goddess Nemhain.

Nemhain's involvement in such battles reinforces my earlier argument that Myrddin's/Merlin's Lady of the Lake – who goes by names such as Viviane, Ninniane, Nimiane, etc., and who is also found in Welsh sources as Nefyn, wife of Cynfarch – is indeed Nemhain.

So what to make of Myrddin's madness?

Part of the clue to solving the mystery may involve the 'coincidental' pairings of Myrddin/Llallogan and St. Martin and/or St. Ninian sites. We find early St. Martin churches in Liddesdale, where Myrddin fights and is defeated at Arfderydd/Arderydd. We find St. Ninian (of Whithorn or Candida Casa, with its supposed very early St. Martin's Church) at Cathures (probably the Roman fort of Cadder) and at the Molendinar Burn in Glasgow, where St. Kentigern later met Llallogan (Laloecen). We find a Martin name atop Myrddin's mountain of Tinto, and there was a Ninian church at Wiston itself (although this appears to have been established by the Templers).

Some have tried to make a case for Myrddin BEING St. Martin, but, in Welsh, Martinus would become *Merthin, and it is impossible, linguistically speaking, for Myrddin to come from the Latin name. To quote Professor Ranko Matasovic on this fact:

> "Phonologically, Martin (Lat. Martinus) cannot correspond to W. Myrddin. What you get from Lat. Martinus in Welsh is Marthin (cf. the place-name Llanfarthin in Shropshire). However, one cannot exclude the possibility that the similarity of the two names contributed to their confusion, say, that Sanctus Martinus became Myrddin."

Or, as seems most likely, the Christian Martin merely replaced the Pagan Myrddin at the latter's sacred sites. This would be in keeping with standard Christian practice of the time, which sought to build churches and shrines over the remains of earlier Pagan holy places.

Myrddin Llallawg/Llallogan, Gwyllon, Ellyllon and the Chwyfleian: The Land of the Dead Beyond Hadrian's Wall.

The 'madness' of Myrddin is, in reality, a spectral state. I've written at length about this elsewhere, so I will not repeat what

I've said before. But I would like to briefly address the significance of divine spirits of the dead in the context of our exploration of Myrddin's nature and character.

One of the most important early sources to mention the prevalence of the dead north of Hadrian's Wall is that of Procopius's *History of the Wars*, 8.20.42-8:

> "Now in this island of Britain the men of ancient times built a long wall, cutting off a large part of it; and the climate and the soil and everything else is not alike on the two sides of it. For to the south of the wall there is a salubrious air, changing with the seasons, being moderately warm in summer and cool in winter. But on the north side, everything is the reverse of this, so that it is actually impossible for a man to survive there even a half-hour, but countless snakes and serpents and every other kind of wild creature occupy this area as their own. And, strangest of all, the inhabitants say that if a man crosses this wall and goes to the other side, he dies straightaway. They say, then, that the souls of men who die are always conveyed to this place."

In isolation, this statement seems bizarre, even silly. But if we look at the early Myrddin poetry (and the Suibhne Geilt material on the Irish side of things), it becomes evident that wild areas in Celtic belief were the home of ghostly 'wild men'. And the extensive forest of the Scottish Lowlands, the haunt of Myrddin, was just such a place.

We cannot know how much this belief was influenced by the Romans, who deified their own dead. The common formula 'D M' on Roman tombstones is, perhaps, the best example of such a practice. I asked Professor Roger Tomlin his thoughts on this, and he was kind enough to provide me with the following response:

> "I hope I am not over-simplifying it ... but DIS is an adjective, dative plural, contracted from DIVIS ('divine'), which of

course is also the substantive DIVUS (a 'god', especially a deified emperor). MANES (plural) are the spirits of the dead, regarded as minor deities. So a tombstone is a dedication to 'the divine dead' collectively, 'the Shades of the Dead'. If SACRVM is added, it refers to the tombstone, or at least to the act of dedication 'to' the Manes.

The god of the Underworld is DIS PATER, which I take to be 'Father' DIVUS contracted (or at least a cognate word). He is equated with Pluto, Hades, etc.; however, tombstones are not dedicated to him, but to the Divine Shades, the DI MANES.

Like us, the Romans found this difficult, since they are often unsure whether to follow D M with the deceased name in the genitive, as if it were 'his' Manes, or in the dative, as if it were a dedication to him too."

Perhaps the most important part of Procopius's story is where he says the dead were conveyed to the region north of the wall. Conveyance implies a conveyor, and in Greek and Roman religions such a divinity was known as a 'psychopomp'. The Roman psychopomp was Mercury, and it is Mercury who was identified with the god Lugus, the Welsh Lleu. I and others have drawn strong parallels between Myrddin and the god Lleu. At one time, I was convinced Myrddin either was Lleu or a Lleu-avatar.

Below I have drawn the more important words connected with ghosts and wild men from the *GPC*. My readers may wish to check the definitions for these words and draw their own conclusions as to how such words may have come to be applied to the spirits of the dead.

I would also hasten to add that there may have been a god named Alletios at Corbridge on Hadrian's Wall. His name derives from the same root as the Welsh words *ellyll*, *llall* and that of Myrddin's nickname Llallawg/Llallogan. Here is what I have on Alletios, drawn from a couple of previous essays:

Dr. Graham Isaac, now with the National University of Ireland, Galway, commented as follows on this place-name:

"The form of the name Elleti is corroborated by the instance of 'palude [Latin for 'marsh' or 'swamp'] Elleti' in the *Book of Llan Dav* (p148). But since both that and HB's campum Elleti are in Latin contexts, we cannot see whether the name is OW Elleti (= Elledi) or OW Ellet (= Elled) with a Latin genitive ending. Both are possible. My guess would be that OW Elleti is right – as the W suffix -i would motivate affection, so allowing the base to be posited as all-, the same as in W. *ar-all* 'other', *all-tud* 'exile', Gaulish *allo-*, etc. Elleti would be 'other-place, place of the other side (of something)'."

If Isaac is right, we are fortunate in that Elleti may be found in the form of a personal name at the Corbridge Roman fort on Hadrian's Wall. A fragment of a large grey urn was found there, bearing the name 'ALLIITIO' (Fascicule 8, RIB 2502.9; information courtesy of Georgina Plowright, Curator, English Heritage Hadrian's Wall Museum). This could be the potter's name, perhaps a form of the nomen Alletius, or the name of the god portrayed on the fragment. J. Leach (in *The Smith God in Roman Britain*, Archaeologia Aeliana, 40, 1962, pp.171-184) made a case for the god in question being a divine smith, primarily due to the presence on the urn fragment of what appears to be an anvil in relief, although there were also metal workings in the neighbourhood of Corbridge. Anne Ross (in her *Pagan Celtic Britain*, p253) associates the name Allitio with the same all-, 'other', root that Dr. Isaac linked to Elleti. She thinks Allitio may have been a warrior/smith-god, and very tentatively offers 'God of the Otherworld' for this theonym.

On the name 'ALLIITIO', Dr. Isaac agrees with Ross:

"Taking the double -ll- at face value, as I would be inclined to do as a working hypothesis, that would be connected to the W. *all-* that I have mentioned before."

It may be worth noting that the divine name Allitio – again, according to Dr. Isaac – can be associated with Myrddin's/Merlin's Welsh nickname, Llallogan or Llallawc. This last derives from Proto-Celtic *alal(I)yo- 'another, other', cf. Old Irish *arail*, Middle Welsh *arall* (OW and MW), Middle Breton *al(l)all*, *arall*, Cornish *arall*. This is a reduplicated, intensive variant of Proto-Celtic *al(I)yo- 'other', cf. Old Irish *aile* [io], Middle Welsh *eil*, *all-*, Middle Breton *eil*, Cornish *yl*, Gaulish *Allo-broges*, *allos*, Proto-Indo-European *h2elyo- 'other', Latin alius, Go. *aljis*. Celtic-Iberian *ailam*, which has been interpreted as the Acc. of this pronoun, has also been taken to mean something like 'place, abode'.

Treating more fully of 'ALLIITIO' in a private communication, Georgina Plowright, Curator, English Heritage Hadrian's Wall Museum, says that the name "… occurs twice on one piece of pottery showing feet and a base. This is always assumed to be the base of an anvil, with the feet being those of a smith god. There are a number of sherds of grey pottery from Corbridge with very distinctive applied decoration, with two recognisable themes: the smith god shown with hammer and anvil, and a wheel god who is shown with wheel and club. The fact that the wheel god is depicted by a mould suggests that this type of pottery was being made at Corbridge, though it appears on a number of other sites. The reading occurs twice on this piece of pottery: once in the frame created by the anvil base, and then on the pot below the feet of the standing figure. Another sherd showing the smith god does not have any inscription. John Dore and Stephen Johnson, who did the captions for the Corbridge gallery, have assumed that the name might be that of a potter, though *RIB* seems to go for either god or potter. I haven't got a copy of the Leach reference easily to hand, but my memory tells me the item should be illustrated there."

For an online article that mentions the 'Allitio' found at Corbridge, please see: http://romanpotterystudy.org/new/wp-content/uploads/ 2015/07/JRPS-2-Webster-2-28.pdf

MYRDDIN: THE CULT OF THE DEAD VS. THE CULT OF THE SAINTS

"Seven score men of rank became Wild Ones,
In the forest of Celyddon they perished ..."
—from *The Dialogue of Merlin and Taliesin*
(in *The Black Book of Carmarthen*).

Many years ago, I realized that Myrddin's madness at the Battle of Arderydd was a metaphor for a spectral state of existence following the death of the body. This led me to believe that Myrddin was a sort of revered ghost, something akin to the Manes of Roman religion. About the closest thing we in the modern world can compare this to is the Cult of the Saints. We understand how a dead holy man could be worshiped, and how one could communicate with him.

The primary difference between the two is that while a saint became divine after his death due to his religious works in life, a Pagan became a species of god simply because ghosts were inherently divine.

The problem with Myrddin has always been whether to simply view him as a mortal who has gone mad (or died) or as a demoted god. The triple death meted out to him has led scholars to associate him with the god Lugh (or Mars Condate; see https://mistshadows.blogspot.com/2020/03/myrddin-mars-condatis-and-st-martin.html) or a trio of continental divinities (see Anne Ross and Don Robins' *The Life and Death of a Druid Price*). Of course, a man sacrificed to a god, in a very strange way, becomes the god – at least, symbolically. Whether it was believed he actually became 'one' with the god is not known. We may compare the sacrifice of a Viking to the Norse Odin, who hung, like the god, from a tree. If any god is involved with Myrddin, it would appear (due to his constant association in place-names with Ninian/Finnian) to be Gwyn, the god of the dead in Welsh tradition (see https://mistshadows.blogspot.com/2020/05/myrddin-st-ninian-st-martin-and-white.html). But as Gwyn had in his train the legion of the dead, Myrddin may simply have been one of these spirits. He was replaced by St. Martin, due not only to a superficial resemblance of their names but also because St. Martin died on the date of a Roman festival to the Manes and his feast/funeral day became known as Old Halloween or Old Allhallows Eve.

Geoffrey of Monmouth muddied the waters even more. He has Ganieda/Gwenddydd (who would seem to be a Welsh form of Diana) build Merlin/Myrddin an 'observatory' – which is plainly a megalithic structure similar to the Stonehenge he later has Merlin build. The implication is that he should be seen as a manifestation of Apollo or, at the very least, a priest of the sun god. He identifies Merlin with Ambrosius, so Merlin becomes the character in the famous story of the red and white dragons. Ambrosius's origin at Campus Elleti is changed to Carmarthen, and his Guoloph becomes Galabes. And he incorporates other themes, such as having Merlin transform Uther into Gorlois (when in the Welsh Uther elegy poem the chieftain calls himself Gorlassar and is transformed by God). He has Merlin lead an army of stags (which I thought might be Carvetii warriors, a people who worshiped a god called Mars Belatucadros). The contestants at Arderydd are assigned to the wrong kingdoms. The triple death is prophesied by Merlin, but belongs to another character. Merlin goes in and out of madness and we are left wondering whether this is supposed to imply a seasonal rebirth-death cycle or is nothing more than imaginative storytelling. Finally, he brings into Merlin's story all kinds of Classically derived names and motifs, and even nuggets of Irish mythology (all the names of the goddesses of Avalon cited by Merlin are Irish in origin). So, what we end up with, essentially, is an eclectic mess, well-nigh immune to dissection and forensics. It is, admittedly, a work of creative genius. But it does not follow that Merlin was originally anything like how he is portrayed in *The Life of Merlin* and *The History of the Kings of Britain* – sources that utterly contradict each other.

In my opinion, as is true when we are searching for an historical Arthur, we must dispense with Geoffrey of Monmouth's works entirely if we hope to uncover anything of real value in terms of a Myrddin prototype.

The fragments concerning Lailocen (Welsh Llallogan; cf. Llalog) in *The Life of St. Kentigern* are of an entirely different order. In one, the 'wild man' is placed at an early St. Ninian/Finnian site in Glasgow (Molendinar Burn) [as the Welsh poetry situates Myrddin on the mountain of Abercarf/Tinto/Wiston with its chapel of St. Ninian and Martingill Cleuch]. In the other, the triple death is relocated from the Willow Pool confluence of the Liddel (with its tributary the Tweed/Tweeden) and Esk to the confluence of the Powsail ('Willow Pool') and the Tweed. Close to the former is the St. Martin's Church at Canonbie.

The easiest way for us to understand Myrddin is to take a good look at a recent study of the Roman cult of the dead by Dr. Charles King. After offering a definition of the Manes, the author challenges "the widespread assumption that the term 'Manes' always refers to collective groups of the dead" and demonstrates "that the Romans worshipped dead individuals as Manes."

I urge my readers to consult *The Ancient Roman Afterlife: Di Manes, Belief, and the Cult of the Dead*.

The strictly Pagan worship of the dead – as it, obviously, involved the worship of dead Pagans – would have been seen as highly objectionable by the Christian Church. It was, though, of a different magnitude than trying to grapple with the problem posed by a more powerful Pagan god. In some cases, Pagan deities were 'converted' into saints. The best example of this in the Celtic world is probably Brigid of Ireland. But, what to do with a deified Pagan mortal?

However, Finnbar of Cork (who, like Myrddin, is associated with a sacred apple tree; Moville designates a sacred tree) bears a name which is reminiscent of that belonging to the Connacht King of the Fairies, Finnbheara/Fionnbharr (and other variants). From the *Oxford Dictionary of Celtic Mythology*:

"King of the Connacht fairies with residence at Cnoc Mheada [Knockmagha], west of Tuam, Co. Galway. Although fond of mortal women, he is usually cited with his wife Úna (sometimes Nuala). Originally one of the Tuatha Dé Danann, he settles at Cnoc Mheadha when his kind are driven underground by the Milesians. The popularity of his stories in oral tradition led storytellers to think of Finnbheara as the king of all Irish fairies, not just of Connacht, and also as king of the dead. In one of the best-known stories, Finnbheara steals the most beautiful woman in Ireland, Eithne or Eithne the Bride, and keeps her with him, Persephone-like, for a year. He brings good crops to people in his region but his absence brings poor crops. He rewards a smith who is not afraid to shoe his three-legged horse. On one occasion he cures a sick woman, accepts food from her in recompense, but refuses salt. Lady Wilde collected many stories of Finnbheara in her *Ancient Legends, Mystic Charms and Superstitions of Ireland* (London, 1887). T.H. Nally's verse pantomime *Finn Varra Maa* (Dublin, 1917) conflates Finnbheara with Fionn mac Cumhaill (here 'Finn MacCool') and makes him the Irish Santa Claus. W.B. Yeats cites him often, usually as Finvara, notably in the dramas *The Land of Heart's Desire* (1894) and *The Dreaming of the Bones* (1919). Although his name is occasionally anglicized as Finbar, he should be distinguished from Finnbarr" (Folk motifs: F109; F160.0.2; F167.12; F184; F252.1).

I've elsewhere discussed the Welsh Gwyn as God of the dead, and his probable identification with the Irish Fionn and Apollo Vindonnus (https://mistshadows.blogspot.com/2020/05/myrddin-st-ninian-st-martin-and-white.html).

Myrddin, then, as 'Elf-man', was a sort of British King of the Fairies who came to be identified with his Irish counterpart. The Christian Martin replaced him in the landscape, but not in the minds of those who believed in him. I would add that St. Finnbar of Cork resided at Templemartin (https://www.logainm.ie/en/685). While I've not been able to determine how old the Templemartin name is, it would not be strange if a foundation of a Finnbar in Galloway may have been designated a St. Martin chapel in memory of the Irish place-name.

A final note on Myrddin's triple death ... The original story may have had Myrddin die (possibly of panic; Irish war goddesses could kill with that alone) at Arderydd. But because his spectral state was misunderstood, it was thought necessary to 'tag on' a proper death to his story. On the other hand, I have proposed that the triple death was a human sacrifice meant to ensure victory in the upcoming battle. Such a sacrifice would have gone beyond deifying Myrddin as a simple ancestral ghost. As I've alluded to above, sacrifice victims symbolized the god himself and, in a way that is hard to understand, became that god. So, the very act of dying in a sacrificial rite may have, essentially, 'enthroned' Myrddin as King of the Fairies. In essence, once he passed over to the Otherworld, he was the god of the dead.

As the Irish King of the Fairies ruled from the hill of Knockmagha, Myrddin seems to have had his 'court' at Tinto, atop which is one of the largest Bronze Age burial cairns in all of Scotland (https://canmore.org.uk/site/47525/tinto-cairn). It was there that he communed with the 'wild men' (ghosts). Graham Isaac has, undoubtedly, correctly rendered Myrddin's father's name Morfryn as 'Elf-hill', and this may well be a designation for Tinto.

ARDERYDD/ARMTERID/ARFDERYDD AND ARTHURET, CUMBRIA

Over the years, I've explored different possibilities for the location of the famous Armterid/Arfderydd battle, at which Merlin (Myrddin) went mad and fled into the Caledonian Wood. But only recently have I been able to settle on one particular site.

The place was called 'Weapon-fierce' (courtesy of Andrew Breeze https://digitalcommons.brockport.edu/jlo/vol2/iss1/1/), i.e. Arm-terid or Arf-derydd. According to Breeze, this was the name for the stream at Carwinley which marked the northern boundary of Arthuret parish.

As for fixing the site of the battle, we have one possible clue. In *Lailoken and Kentigern*, Carwinley or Caer Gwenddolau is called Carwannock, and the battle is said to take place between the latter and the Liddel on a plain. I had proposed that -wannock was either derived from Cumbric *gwaun*, 'high and wet level ground, moorland, heath, low-lying marshy ground, meadow', or might be a hypocoristic form of Gwenddolau. Gwen-ddolau itself looks to be a place-name, as it means, literally, 'White dales' (*dol* being 'meadow, dale, field, pasture, valley'). Brythonic place-name expert Alan James confirmed both possibilities for me:

> "The meaning of derivatives of *$w\bar{a}gn\bar{a}$ in the Brittonic languages is primarily 'level, marshy ground', whether upland or lowland; developments include *gwaun* 'a meadow' in Welsh, and *goon* 'downland, unenclosed pasture' in Cornish. Br -āco-/ā-> -ǫg is an adjectival and nominal suffix, indicating 'being of the kind of', 'association with', 'abounding in', the stem-word. It occurs very widely in river-names, hill-names and other topographic names. It's not diminutive, though in hypocoristic personal names like Gwennock it might be affectionate."

Thus Carwannock and Carwinley are the same place. This is confirmed, in fact, by the primary sources. In the St. Kentigern VITA fragment (Titus A. XIX ff. 74-75b) the language is in campo qui est inter Lidel et Carwannock (see https://www.persee.fr/doc/roma_0035-8029_1893_num_22_88_5789). But according to the fifteenth-century edition of John of Fordun, the battle took place in campo inter Lidel et Carwanolow situato (Ifor Williams quoted in PNCmb I p51 n1).

But what of modern Arthuret, which is considerably to the south of Carwinley? Derydd as similar to L. torridus, 'dried up', also Irish *tioradh*, 'drying', *tíraid*, 'dries'. Guess what is a tributary of the Hall Burn in Arthuret parish?

The Dry Beck (see http://www.lakesguides.co.uk/html/lgaz/lk00252.htm).

So this stream is Terydd/Derydd – probably the original name for the entire Hall Burn, which flows past Arthuret proper.

The question is then, what is Arm-/Arf-? Although almost all sources had Ard- and not Arf-, I'm aware of the lectio difficilior requirement here. So, what is Arf-/Arm-?

There is Gaelic *airm*, 'place', and that has been proposed, but it's really not very convincing, given its total absence otherwise in Britain. From Alan James' *BLITON*:

*arμ (f?)
Early Celtic *armā- > Br *armā-; O MIr, G *airm*.
'Place, location, whereabouts'.

Proposed by I. Williams, see PNCmb pp.51–2, in [bellum] Armterid AC573 (in London, BL MS Harley 3859). There is no other evidence for the word in P-Celtic, nor does the Goidelic form seem to occur as a place-name generic. If a Brittonic cognate had existed and survived, it would have fallen together as it did in Goidelic with adopted Lat arma 'arms' (Welsh *arf*). See Arthuret Cmb, below.

a2) The river-name Armet Water MLo (Stow), PNMLo p75, SPN² p241, and the territorial name Armethe Stg (Muiravonside), PNFEStg p38, could formally be + -ed if adopted early enough by Northumbrian Old English speakers to retain –m- (LHEB §§98–100, pp.486–93); however, such a formation would be unlikely to involve *arμ. An early hydronymic element is possible, see *ERN* p149 (discussion of R. Erme Dev), and *ar* in river-names.

b2) Arthuret Cmb PNCmb pp.51–2 ? + -*tērïð. Arthuret church stands on a prominent bluff overlooking the Border Esk about two miles south of Longtown. Williams' identification of the battle-site with Arthuret is plausible, given the strategic location, though it should not be regarded as certain. On the burgeoning of stories surrounding this battle in medieval Welsh literature, see Rowlands (1990), pp.109–14. See also discussion of Carwinley under *cajr*.

I have long maintained that the Arm-/Arf- spelling is a poetic development and does not represent a real place-name. After extensive discussion with Dr. Simon Rodway of The University of Wales, I've gotten agreement on this point. In addition, I had proposed that the Arderydd 'variant' might derive from either Ar-derydd, 'in front of the Derydd' or Ardd-derydd, 'the height of the Derydd'. This last seemed the most reasonable to me, as the rotwyd or rhodwydd Arderys [sic] was a circular, earthen dyke fortification guarding a ford. This is discussed by Bromwich in her *Triads* and by Sir Ifor Williams in a note to his *Taliesin* edition. At Arthuret, this fortification was atop the hill, adjacent to the ford over the River Esk.

The actual origin of rhodwydd is debated. Ifor Williams thought it from *rhawd* + *gwydd*. But I think the *GPC* now has it right, with *rhod* from the word for 'wheel', and *gwydd* being the same as in *gwydd4*, 'tumulus', cf. *gwyddfa*, 'height, eminence, promontory'. Here is what Dr. Rodway had to say on the subject:

"I think the best explanation is *Ardd-derydd < *Ardo-torridus – both variants can derive from this, and there would be good motivation for alteration in order to avoid a car crash of dentals following syncope of the composition vowel. (1) Arfderydd: *dd* and *f* sometimes interchange, e.g. *afanc* ~ *addanc*. (2) Arderydd fricatives can be lost after *r* in post-syncope consonant clusters. Analogy could have played a part in both forms – as it was famous as the site of a battle, *arf* 'weapon' might have seemed appropriate, and for Arderydd we have plenty of place-names containing *ar* 'in front of, opposite', e.g. Arfon, Arberth, etc."

Thus, the location of the Arderydd battle was the 'dry' stream at Arthuret.

For the best discussion of the actual fortification at Arthuret, consult W.F. Skene's *Notice of the Site of the Battle of Ardderyd or Arberyth*. https://archaeologydataservice.ac.uk/archiveDS/archiveDownload?t=arch-352-1/dissemination/pdf/vol_006/6_091_098.pdf:

"About a mile south from Longtown is the church and rectory of Arthuret, situated on a raised platform on the west side of the river Esk, which flows past them at a lower level; and south of the church and parsonage there rises from this platform two small hills covered with wood, called the Arthuret knowes. The top of the highest, which overhangs the river, is fortified by a small earthen rampart, enclosing a space nearly square, and measuring about sixteen yards square."

Do note, however, that Skene was wrong to look towards the Moat of Liddel as the actual site of Arderydd. Liddel Strength, as it is otherwise known, is over a kilometer north of the northern boundary of Arthuret parish and is, needless to say, nowhere near the Dry Beck.

THE 'ROTWYD' (RHODWYDD) OF ARDERYS (ARDERYDD)

The early Welsh poetry on Arfderydd mentions something called the 'rotwyd' or rhodwydd. Scholars cannot say exactly what this was, but they have made a good guess. According to Rachel Bromwich (see her text, translation and commentary on *The Triads of the Island of Britain*):

> "... Rhodwydd can mean either a ford or an earthen dyke; the latter was frequently constructed on rising ground above a ford, and would be held instead of the ford itself. This was often the place where the fiercest battles were fought."

Sir Ifor Williams (in his notes to *The Poems of Taliesin*) adds:

> "... these examples show that *rhyd* (ford) and *rhodwydd* occur together often, and Loth suggested that *rhodwydd* was synonymous with *rhyd* ... *Rhodwydd* may be from *rhawd* [cognate with Irish *rath*, 'ringfort, earthen fortification'; cf. *beddrod*, *bed* + *rhawd*] and *gwydd*, cf. *gwydd-fa* [height, eminence, promontory; seat, throne, mound, burial ground, grave, burial mound, etc., where *gwydd* = grave, burial mound, grave, burial mound, tumulus]."

As Arthuret in Cumbria is an esker/ridge that anciently was much closer the Esk, and there was once an ancient earthwork atop this ridge, we could assume that the 'rotwyd' of Arderydd is a reference to this very earthwork which may have once stood guard over a ford on the river.

EARLY WELSH TRADITION VERSUS JOCELYN'S LIFE OF KENTIGERN: A SECOND DEATH FOR MYRDDIN AND A CHRISTIAN BURIAL

For years now, I've been unable to reconcile what I perceive to be two separate strands in the early Myrddin (= Merlin) tradition. The first concerns the death of a warrior or chieftain (or god; see my discussion of Lugh below) named Llallogan in a battle at Arderydd/Arthuret and his wandering the woods as a disembodied spirit, his spectral state being misunderstood by a later age as a state of madness. This version of the story is implicit in the early Welsh sources. The second story is from *The Life of St. Kentigern*. There, Myrddin the madman wanders the woods until he eventually meets his triple sacrificial death at the hands of Meldred's shepherds at Drumelzier on the Tweed.

Drumelzier was known anciently as Dunmeller, the 'oppidum Dunmeller' of *The Life of St. Kentigern*. The best modern philologists can do with the name, in its various early spellings, is din-, 'fort', plus –medal- plus –wir, plural of wur, cf. W. *medalwyr*, 'reapers', in the metaphorical sense of warriors.

The name Meldred appears to be an anachronism, as Meldredus is a known form of the much later historical Maldred, sometimes-styled son of Crinan the Thane. It used to be accepted that this Crinan was to be identified with Crinan the lay-abbot of Dunkeld, the 'Fort of the Caledonians'. But much doubt has been cast upon this identification by recent scholars. See, for example, the discussion of the problem in *Saints' Cults in the Celtic World* (by Steve Boardman, John Reuben Davies and Eila Williamson, Boydell Press, 2013).

According to Alex Woolf at the University of St. Andrews:

"All we really know about him [Maldred] comes from the text known as *De obsessione Dunelmensis* which simply says that a daughter of Earl Uhtred married a certain Maldred son of Crinan the Thegn, a very rich man, by whom she gave birth to Cospatric. Cospatric was the Earl of Northumbria just after the Norman Conquest. We know nothing about the location of Maldred or his father, unless we assume the father is Crinan of Dunkeld.

There was a Gospatric who was Lord of Allerdale c.1060, and a Dolphin (possibly brother of Gospatric) who controlled Carlisle c.1090. The Earl of Northumbria c.1070 was Gospatric son of Maldred. The people who make Maldred Lord of Allerdale and Carlisle presume the Gospatric(s) mentioned in relation to them was Gospatric son of Maldred (which is possible but not certain) and they are assuming he inherited his position. This latter seems less likely, since *De Obsessione* tells us that Gospatric son of Maldred's claim to high status, and ultimately the earldom, was through his mother, not his father. Dolphin being in Carlisle is mentioned only once in the *Anglo-Saxon Chronicle* and in no other source. Scottish charters of the early twelfth century are sometimes witnessed by someone described as 'Gospatric brother of Dolphin'. Gospatric son of Maldred was the Earl of Northumbria who fled to Scotland. His descendants eventually became earls of Dunbar, but we don't know if he is the same person as Gospatric of Allerdale."

It is possible that Meldred/Maldred was placed at Drumelzier because of the presence there of Thane's Castle (now Tinnis Castle). Alternately, Meldred may have been placed at Dunmeller merely as a sort of folk etymology, with the place-name being fancifully derived from the personal name. Alan James believes this to be a very real possibility. I would also mention that Jocelyn, who wrote *Kentigern's Life*, was based at Furness in Cumbria, so there may have been a political element to his choosing Maldred for the Lailoken story.

The etymology of the name Maldred is unknown. Alex Woolf tentatively offers an English garbling of the Irish *Mael Doraid*. Oliver Padel thinks the first element should be from British *Maglo-, 'prince, lord, ruler'. I once proposed *Mael + drud* for 'Bold Prince', although I noted that the Irish cognate to Welsh *drud – druth* – meant 'fool', and that this reminded us of Jocelyn calling Lailoken "homo fatuus", 'foolish man'. We could perhaps derive the name from Mael + derydd, for a meaning of something like 'Ardent/Fierce Prince'.

Attempts have been made to find Myrddin's grave not at the Drumelzier in Tweeddale, but at the similarly named place near Dunipace in Stirlingshire. The most elaborate argument for placing Myrddin's death-place at the Drumelzier on the Carron has been produced by Adam Ardrey his book, *Finding Merlin: The Truth Behind the Legend*. Mr. Ardrey's website may be found here: http://finding-merlin.com/.

It is true that this second Drumelzier appears to be an ancient name. To quote from Zoe Ellis, Archives Assistant with the Falkirk Community Trust (personal correspondence):

> "Drumelzier, also known as Drumalzier, is an ancient name. It appears on the first series Ordnance Survey map (published in 1865) as Drimallier, and was still called Drimallier on a 1951 OS map. It also appears on Roy's military survey map of Scotland (done in the 1750s) as Drumalzierst.
>
> In the Archives, we have a copy of a book called *The Place Names of Falkirk and East Stirlingshire* by John Reid. This book notes that the earliest written references to Drumelzier (from 1608) refer to it as 'Drummelzarislandis' or Drumelzier's-lands, and the book therefore suggests that the lands may have had the same name as their owner. It doesn't speculate further on the derivation of the name itself."

The reason for looking at this second Drumelzier is, primarily, because Myrddin's grave as described in Tweeddale cannot now be found. CANMORE nicely summarizes the problem of this missing grave:

> "Merlin's Grave (Site): According to legend which is at least as old as the fifteenth century, the wizard Merlin was buried 200 yds NNW of Drumelzier Church, on the level haugh close to the right bank of the River Tweed. No structural remains are now to be seen, or have ever been recorded, at the place in question, but it is possible that the tradition may have originated from the discovery of a Bronze Age cist.
> RCAHMS 1967, visited 1956.
> There is nothing to be seen at this site which lies in a field. The tradition still survives.
> Visited by OS(IA) 11th August, 1972."

The idea, then, is that one of the Hills of Dunipace was a barrow mound or had a grave incorporated into it, and that the Tweeddale Drumelzier is simply the wrong one. I've noted before that St. Ninian, whose establishment is close to Plean, is often brought into connection with Myrddin because of the former's association with St. Martin. Might there be something to the Dunipace connection?

No. The legend that places Merlin's grave on the river is simply wrong. The earliest account of where he was buried is in *The Life of St. Kentigern*, and there we are plainly told by Merlin himself that:

> "I want you to bury me in the eastern part of the city in the churchyard, where the faithful are interred, not far from the green chapel where the brook Pausayl [now the Drumelzier Burn] flows into the River Tweed ..."

There was never a Powsail Burn at or near Dunipace. The 'green chapel' here, of course, is another matter and will be discussed in more detail below. For now, suffice it to say that it could be a description of a barrow mound or cairn (cf. the green chapel in *Sir Gawain and the Green Knight*) which has been eroded away by the river over the past centuries. But the important thing to note is that we are not told Merlin was buried in the green chapel. He is said to have been buried in the churchyard.

The present Drumelzier Kirk is not very old, but it probably stood upon the spot of an earlier, more ancient establishment. Whether we can identify the modern churchyard with the ancient one is not something that can ever be determined.

But why Drumelzier at all? If I am right and the sacrifice of Merlin at the hands of Meldred's shepherds is merely a story invented to both Christianize him and provide him with a death-tale (the actual nature of his madness being misunderstood), then why was this location on the Tweed chosen?

Principally, for two reasons. I mentioned above that the great Dreva Craig hillfort on the opposite side of the Tweed from Drumelzier has very near it a hill called Louden Knowe. Scottish place-name expert John Wilkinson helpfully provides the following information online (http://johngarthwilkinson.com/2014/lanum-and-lugudunum/):

> "Louden Knowe PEB [NT 137363], an outlier of Trahenna Hill, sits at the head of a long ridge above the magnificently situated hillfort known nowadays as Dreva Craig (where Dreva is a farm and Drev- will reflect W *tref* 'steading' in a hilly and isolated area which shelters many extant Cumbric place-names), long famous for its chevaux de frise (R. Feachem, *Guide to Prehistoric Scotland*, London, 1963; Second Edition 1977, p143); across from Drumelzier on the middle reaches of the Tweed (where a legend of Merlin/ Myrddin as Lailoken is localised), it may preserve another

*Lugudunon. Thanks to Bill Patterson for finding the name (not on the OS 1:50,000 Landranger)."

For more information on the exact location of this hill, see:

https://scotlandsplaces.gov.uk/digital-volumes/ordnance-survey-name-books/peeblesshire-os-name-books-1856-1858/peeblesshire-volume-39/25

Brythonic place-name expert Alan James agrees with Wilkinson on the etymology for Louden (personal communication).

As Myrddin has strong affinities with the god Lleu (see below), his placement at Drumelzier, opposite Llue's fort, need not surprise you.

The second reason Myrddin's death may have been transferred from Arderydd/Arthuret to Drumelzier on the Tweed doubtless has to do with the presence of the Tweeden Burn in Liddesdale at Newcastleton. The Tweeden Burn empties into the Liddel Water.

Early forms of this stream-name include Tueeden (Blaeu/Pont Map, 1654), Tweden (1541, 1580, and 1583), Tueden (1599), and Twyden (1841).

According to Alan James, this stream-name appears to represent Tweed + a diminutive Brittonic –in suffix, and this:

> "... pushes the name back to the twelfth century or earlier, possibly a lot earlier, and implies the stream was called Tweed or something similar before that."

Given that Myrddin/Llallogan fought at Arthuret where the Liddel and the Esk meet, and Meldred/Maldred may have been the Lord of Cumbria, I would identify as the proper death-place of our 'madman' the Tweeden Burn. This notion is made all the more attractive by the presence at Old Castleton, a bit further up the Liddel, of a very early St. Martin's Church, quite possibly an establishment originating from Whithorn. I have suggested elsewhere that Myrddin was either identified with St. Martin or replaced by the saint in several locations in Lowland Scotland.

If I am correct and the Tweeden Burn is the place where Myrddin underwent his triple sacrifice, then the churchyard he was buried in must be that of St. Martin's at Old Castleton. Note that there is no St. Martin or St. Ninian connection to Drumelzier.

However, we have forgotten about the Powsail Burn at Drumelzier. This place-name is from *pol-, 'pool', plus the word for 'willow'. Not coincidentally, there is a Willow Pool at the confluence of the Liddel Water and the Esk. This is also the location of the Liddel Strength fort, sometimes also referred to in the sources as the Moat of Liddel (not to be confused with the castle at Old Castleton in Liddesdale).

For years now, I have accepted the most recent translation 'green chapel' for the edifice that supposedly stands near where Myrddin/Merlin is buried. However, knowing as I do all too well the freedom translators can take when rendering medieval Latin, I went to the source and checked it out myself.

The most recent version of the relevant passage drawn from the *Vita Kentigern* was done by a Zacharias P. Thundy and is found in Peter Goodrich's *The Romance of Merlin*. It reads:

> "Lailoken said, 'There is something I very much desire; you can easily grant me that besides my freedom. I want you to bury me in the eastern part of the city in the churchyard, where the faithful are interred, not far from the green chapel where the brook Pausayl flows into the River Tweed, which, indeed, will take place in a few days after my triple death.'"

The actual Latin text is as follows:

> "Respondit Lailoken. vnum valde dabile postulo. libertate non pretermissa. videlicet vt tradas corpus meum sepulture, ad partem huius oppidi orientalem. in loco funeri. fidelis defuncti competenciore, haut longe a cespite. vbi torrens

Passales in flumen descendit Tuedense. Futurum est enim post paucos dies, trina nece me morit[urum]."

What I wanted to know was simply this: where is the 'green chapel' in this Latin?

My understanding of 'cespite' is that is means 'grassy ground, grass, earth, sod, turf, altar/rampart/mound of sod/turf/earth'. It does not mean 'chapel'. It, in fact, must mean a mound of grassy earth, i.e. a barrow mound. So there is no poetic description here of a 'green chapel' – the Latin is quite specific.

Cespite is from caespes, turf, sod, 'used for altars, mounds (of tombs), for covering cottages, huts, etc.'

In brief, a cespite as a grassy mound COULD mean a grave mound. But we also need to bear in mind that the word 'moat', which we now think of as a defensive ditch, often filled with water, is from French via Middle English and during the medieval period it meant MOUND. It was the mound made by scooping dirt out of the surrounding ditch and flinging it up into a gigantic pile, upon which the castle would then be built.

W.F. Skene, in the 1800s, spoke with the farmer at 'Upper Moat', now Highmoat Farm. This is located immediately SW of Liddel Strength, itself often described with the word mote or motte. Willow Pool (= the exact meaning of the Powsail in Tweeddale) is right here at Highmoat. The farmer told Skene that there was a local tradition of Romans and Picts (!) being slain in a great battle and buried in the orchard of Highmoat Farm.

The Tweeden is a major tributary of the Liddel, but it is the Liddel that joins the Willow Pool at the Liddel Strength fortress.

In other words, as I've surmised all along, Myrddin did not survive the Arderydd battle. His madness is a poetic way of describing a post-death spectral state. It usually befell warriors who were frightened to death, but in Myrddin's case it seems to have accompanied his triple sacrifice on the eve of the Arderydd battle.

This spectral state was either not approved of by Christians or was completely misunderstood. In any case, they had to invent a death for him subsequent to the battle and his supposed madness, and then transferred him to what would become, several centuries hence, the Church of Liddel or St. Martin at nearby Canonbie.

Yet the mode of his death – the triple sacrifice – brands him either as the god Lleu or as a sacred Lleu warrior, a sort of Lleu avatar.

The original burial place of Myrddin the 'spectre-man' would appear to have been Highmoat Farm in Cumbria.

THE STORY OF THE STAG: A SEASONAL MYTH?

Geoffrey of Monmouth, in his *Life of Merlin*, tells a very strange tale about Merlin and stags:

"Merlin reads the heavens to learn that his wife Guendoloena (a manufactured feminine form of the personified place-name Gwenddolau, 'White dales') is ready to take another husband in his absence. He seems resigned to this fact, and indeed seems to approve of the match: 'Yet I bear no grudge.' He decides to go to her and give his permission for the marriage to take place, and to bring to her the present he promised her when he left. He then sets off through the woods and clearings, gathering a herd of stags single file, as well as does and she-goats. He seats himself on a stag and drives his ranks of animals before him. He arrives thus at the scene of the wedding and with his stags shouts from the gates for Guendoloena to come out and view her presents. She is astonished that so many wild animals could be brought together and controlled by one man alone. The bridegroom is standing at a high window, and makes the mistake of laughing at Merlin astride his stag-steed. Merlin wrenches the horns off the stag he is mounted upon, whirls them around and throws them at the bridegroom. The bridegroom's head is crushed in and he dies. Then Merlin digs his heels into his mount and it races back towards the woods."

Now, if this story evolved from genuine tradition, the army of stags and does in all likelihood represents a host of Carvetii warriors, as the Carvetii was the 'Stag/Deer tribe'. According to Nicholas Higham and Barri Jones' *The Carvetii* (1991), the original territory of the Carvetii of Cumbria probably extended north and west through the Solway Mosses. This area includes Arthuret. Merlin as leader of the Carvetii would make sense, given what we know about the other combatants at the Battle of Arderydd. In passing, I would remind my reader that the Roman period capital of the Carvetii was Carlisle's fort, Luguvalium. This place-name can either be rendered [the place of] *Luguvalos, a personal name meaning 'Lugh-strong' or – as I prefer – the fort that was 'Lugh-strong'. Such a name for the ruling center of the Carvetii points to the importance of the god Lleu in the region.

The killing of Guendoloena's husband with Myrddin's stag horn has strong mythic overtones, however. This is especially true, as the red deer rut in Cumbria (when stags fight each other for possession of females) reaches its climax in October, and we can be fairly certain, then, that the new chieftain of Arderydd was slain on November 1st or Samhain, the end of the Celtic summer half-year and the beginning of the winter half-year.

After Myrddin kills his rival at Arderydd, he is caught while attempting to flee, bound and handed over to his sister, Ganieda (= Gwenddydd, cf. Goleuddydd; I will propose below that both of these are Welsh names that came to be associated with the Roman Diana Lucina, the moon goddess). Geoffrey makes Ganieda the wife of Rhydderch of Cumbria (not Strathclyde, as was historically accurate). Myrddin is more or less forced to spend some time in human society, but quickly chafes at this and demands to return to his woods. His sister advises him to wait until the 'white winter frosts', soon to be upon the land, have abated. But he rejects her petition and hurries off to the wild. Ganieda builds him a house where he lives during the winter. During the summer, he roams the woods in his role as wild man.

Reading this strictly as a seasonal myth, we have Myrddin as the sun god of the winter half-year, which for the Celts stretched from November 1st to May 1st (Beltaine). The second husband of Guendoloena, killed on November 1st, would be the god of the summer half-year, from May 1st to November 1st. The live god manifests himself as the one who is living with the goddess in her house. The dead god is envisioned as roaming about in the wild as a spectre. Both gods are aspects of the same god, of course, so from story to story, their roles might change.

If I'm interpreting this right, a whole new dimension is added to the motif of Myrddin's madness. Yes, madness is a poetic metaphor for a spectral death-state. However, this madness is not a permanent condition. Seasonal rebirth means an end to the madness/spectral existence. At that point in time, one's 'twin' or solar double dies and, presumably, becomes the 'madman of the wood'.

It may be that this seasonal slaying and rebirth cycle, the becoming alternately mad and sane as mythopoeic language for states of life and death, better explains how Myrddin could perish at the first Arderydd battle, then suddenly reappear later to kill his successor. It would also help explain the triple sacrificial execution meted out to him by Meldred's shepherds – something that was claimed to have occured AFTER his death at Arderydd.

Such an interpretation of Myrddin's madness again brings him more into the realm of the divine than the human. For instance, in Arthurian romance, Lancelot of the Lake, who is none other than the god Lugh Hard-hand, himself goes mad.

As it happens, however, we can actually show with a fair degree of certainly that the god Lleu also took the form of a stag! In the *Mabinogion* tale, *Math Son of Mathonwy*, Lleu's solar twin and rival for the favour of the goddess Blodewedd, Gronw, is depicted as hunting a stag. Blodewedd first sees Gronw during this hunt. The animal is slain at the River Cynfael. Later in the story, Gronw slays Lleu. Once the latter is resurrected from spectral eagle-form by Gwydion, he slays Gronw on the shore of the same river. In mythological language, then, the killing of the stag is a foreshadowing of the killing of Lleu and it is likely that Lleu himself could appear in stag-form.

GWENDDYDD, SISTER OF MYRDDIN

To be honest, this sister of Myrddin has given me fits. Why? Because we know so precious little about her, outside of Geoffrey of Monmouth's fiction.

According to Welsh specialists, her name means 'White Day' (*gwen* is the feminine of *gwyn*, 'white, light, shining, bright, fair'). Geoffrey implies she is the planet and goddess Venus, and that identification has been established in Welsh tradition. But I've also pointed out that she bears a distinct resemblance to the goddess Goleuddydd, 'Light or Brightness of Day', who is married to Cilydd, son of Celyddon Wledig, an eponym for the Celyddon or Caledonian Wood of Myrddin.

I have in the past identified her with the Roman Diana Lucina. As such, she was plainly a lunar goddess, not Venus. I have not changed my mind on this point.

Modern philologists, as well as Romans (see Carin M.C. Green's *Roman Religion and the Cult of Diana at Aricea*, Cambridge University Press, 2007), derive Diana's name from the same root found in Latin dies, 'day', and Diana (like Juno and Hekate) was given the bynames of Lucina, 'the light-bringing' or 'bringing to light' (lucina being, ultimately, from L. lux) and Lucifera, 'light-bringer'. The Vulgate and Post-Vulgate either associate the Lady of the Lake with Diana, or literally identify the two goddesses. This identification came about because the goddess was also Diana Nemorensis, whose shrine was in a wood on Lake Nemi. Her Greek counterpart, Artemis, was called Limnaie/Limnaea, 'of the Lake'.

Cicero, *De Natura Deorum*, 2. 27 (trans. Rackham) (Roman rhetorician, first century B.C.):

> "The name Apollo is Greek; they say that he is the sun, and Diana [Artemis] they identify with the moon ... the name Luna is derived from lucere 'to shine'; for it is the same word as Lucina, and therefore in our country Juno Lucina is invoked in childbirth, as is Diana in her manifestation as Lucifera (the light-bringer) among the Greeks. She is also called Diana Omnivaga (wide-wandering), not from her hunting, but because she is counted as one of the seven planets or 'wanderers' (vagary). She was called Diana because she made a sort of Day (Dia) in the night-time. She is invoked to assist at the birth of children, because the period of gestation is either occasionally seven, or more usually nine, lunar revolutions, and these are called 'menses' (months), because they cover measured (mensa) spaces."

Goleuddydd as wife of the son of Celyddon, who gives birth to Culhwch, the 'Lean Pig', may be an educated reference to the Greek Artemis (= Roman Diana), who sent the Calydonian Boar. One of the primary sub-plots of *Culhwch and Olwen*, of course, is the hunt of the monstrous boar, Twrch Trwyth.

It is also worth noting that when Goleuddydd became pregnant, she went '*gwyll*' – i.e. *gwyllt*, usually defined as 'mad', but more accurately as 'wild' (see *Geiriadur Prifysgol Cymru* for *gwyllt/gwyll*, 'wild, living in a natural or primitive state, uncivilized, savage; demented, raving, frantic, mad), and wandered in uninhabited places. This is also a hallmark of Artemis/Diana the Huntress, who lived in the wilderness. Madness is typically associated with the moon.

Evidence for Diana in Britain during the Roman period can be found in *The Roman Inscriptions of Britain* (see Guy de la Bedoyere site at: romanbritain.freeserve.co.uk/Rbgods.htm):

"Diana.
Auchendavy: altar by M. Cocceius Firmus, centurion of II Augusta. RIB 2174 (with Apollo).
Bath: altar by Vettius B[e]nignus, lib(ertus). RIB 138.
Caerleon: slab recording restoration of a temple of Diana by T. Flavius Postumius [V]arus, senator and (legionary) legate, probably mid-third century if this is the man who was praefectus urbi in Rome in 271 (see RIB). RIB 316.
Corbridge: altar by N[...]. RIB 1126.
Risingham: altar by Aelia Timo. RIB 1209.

Diana Regina.
Newstead: altar by G. Arrius Domitianus, centurion of XX Valeria Victrix. RIB 2122 (see this man again at Newstead under Jupiter Optimus Maximus and Silvanus)."

But if Gwenddydd was indentified with Diana Lucina, why is she located in the far north, in or adjacent to the great Caledonian Wood? Obviously, because Nemorensis (see above) has as its root 'nemus', '(sacred) grove', and so Diana was the goddess of the wood. Coed Celyddon or the 'Wood of Celyddon' was thus a natural place to find the moon goddess.

This does NOT mean that we must allow for Gwenddydd being merely a storyteller's creation. There may certainly have been a purely Celtic moon goddess who was syncretised with the Roman Diana and who was later brought into connection within Gwenddydd.

Both Gwenddydd and the later Arthurian romance Niviane (and variants, i.e. Nemhain/Nefyn) build underworld gravehouses, perhaps with surrounding stone circles for observation of the planets, for Myrddin. Granted, that Gwenddydd did so would seem to rely on the untrustworthy testimony of Geoffrey of Monmouth.

Where is Gwenddydd's house and its adjoining observatory, built for Merlin/Myrddin?

Well, Ryderch (Rodarch) is called by Geoffrey of Monmouth the King of Cumbria, not Strathclyde. This may be a reflection of Carruthers in SE Dumfriesshire. The former is near the Caerlaverock or Lark's Nest said to be the cause of the Arderydd battle. Both are also near ancient settlements and hillforts, as well as the various Mabon place-names found here. At Carruthers is the Birrens Hill settlement, while between the two towns is the mighty Burnswark fort and Roman camp. Riderc or Fort of Rhydderch may be the origin of the family name lying at the root of these town names. A British place-name meaning 'red water' is also a strong candidate, as I have confirmed with Alan James. But regardless of the actual etymology, the site could easily have been taken for a Rhydderch's fort in Welsh tradition. For my recent discussion of the Battle of Arderydd and the Carruthers place-name, see: https://mistshadows.blogspot.com/2019/07/rhydderch-and-missing-urien-new-look-at.html.

Gwenddydd is represented as the sister of Rodarch. If the court of this particular relocated Rhydderch is not to be found in Strathclyde, but here in Dumfriesshire near the border with Cumbria, can we thus extrapolate where Merlin's house and observatory are located?

We are fortunate in possessing an early fourteenth-century elegy by Gwilym Ddu that says Myrddin descended from the tribe of Meirchiaun. This is Meirchiaun Gul of the North, whom I've suggested (in my book, *The Arthur of History*) may belong to the area of Maughanby (earlier 'Meirchiaun's By') in Cumbria, hard by the great Long Meg and Her Daughters stone circle, and only a few miles from the Voreda Roman fort at Old Penrith. This is in the heartland of the ancient Carvetii kingdom.

Meg is a common nickname for Margaret, and the person in question is said to be a seventeenth-century witch – Meg of Meldon. I have wondered whether 'Meg' could be a late substitution for a name similar to that of the ancient Irish goddess Macha, i.e. Imona the horse goddess. Macha was paired with the Morrigan in the same fashion as Nemhain. Voreda can be compared with Welsh *gorwydd*, 'horse' and, according to philologist Kenneth Jackson, means 'Horse stream'.

While Meirchiaun is a Welsh form of the Roman name Marcianus, it may well have been linked to the Welsh plural for horse, viz. *meirch*. The son of Meirchiaun was Cynfarch of the Mote of Mark hillfort in Dumfries. The name Cynfarch means 'chief horse' (cf. Irish *conn* for Cyn-/*Cuno- in this context).

A possible association of Long Meg and Her Daughters with Myrddin is interesting, given the circle's description (from English Heritage's Pastscape website):

> "A stone circle located north of Little Salkeld and east of the River Eden. One of the largest extant stone circles in England, the monument currently comprises 69 large stones, some standing and some fallen, arranged in a flattened oval circa 110 metres by 93 metres. There are two apparent entrances, one to the southwest and the other to the northwest. According to Barnatt, the stones were set in a low bank visible intermittently around the site's circumference except to the north. The enclosure's northern side is 'flattened', i.e. straight rather than curved. Air photography has demonstrated the presence of a large cropmark enclosure (NY 53 NE 21) on this side of the stone circle, and it appears that the stones were here following the

line of the enclosure ditch – at least ten of the stones appear to have stood on the outer lip of the enclosure ditch (which must therefore be earlier than the stone circle). The stone circle's northwest entrance appears to face directly into the entrance of the enclosure. To the southwest of the stone circle, circa 22.5 metres from the southwestern entrance, is a single outlier, an upright red sandstone block some 3.65 metres high known as Long Meg. One face of this boulder is covered with rock art, comprising linear grooves, concentric arcs, spirals, cup marks and grooves. Not all appear finished, and there is some modern graffiti. When viewed from the centre of the circle, Long Meg marks the direction of the midwinter sunset. It has been suggested that two of the stones in the circle's northern arc also feature possible spiral designs. Dating is problematic. No excavations are known to have been undertaken at the site, and a broad later Neolithic/early Bronze Age date would probably encompass both stone circle and rock art. The enclosure NY 53 NE 21 is equally undated, but probably belongs to the same broad time-span.

Like many stone circles, Long Meg and Her Daughters have had a slightly troubled history. A narrow road runs roughly north-south across the eastern half of the circle, and a short distance to the west of this is the line of a former wall. Traces of ridge and furrow are also evident within the circle. In 1599, Camden noted 77 stones, compared to the 69 currently known. William Stukeley subsequently recorded that several stones had been broken up shortly before he visited in 1725. Subsequent accounts also mention the removal and, occasionally, the replacement of stones. Camden also referred to two 'heaps of stone' within the circle. These have been regarded as possible burial mounds, although a later edition of Camden's *Britannia* referred to them as field clearance. In the later seventeenth century, Aubrey referred to 'giants bones, and body' being found within the circle, although there is no confirmation from other sources. Note that Stukeley also referred to a second, smaller circle to the southwest (NY 53 NE 12) of which no trace now remains (13–19)."

This circle sounds suspiciously like the house of seventy doors and as many windows that Myrddin asks his sister Ganieda (Gwenddydd; see below) to build for him in the *Vita Merlini* of Geoffrey of Monmouth. We can visualize the doors as the stone uprights of the circle, and the open spaces between those uprights as the windows. Of course, as Merlin was intimately associated with Stonehenge, it may be that this house of 70 doors and windows is a reference to the latter monument. Just as possible is Myrddin's presence first at Long Meg and Her Daughters, with this stone circle being replaced in folk or literary tradition by the one on Salisbury Plain.

GWENDDYDD/DIANA LUCINA AND NEMHAIN/NEFYN

The moon itself is identified in Scottish lore with Nicnevin, 'Daughter of Nemhain'. Sir Walter Scott, in his *Letters on Demonology and Witchcraft* (1831), describes Nicnevin as follows:

"... a gigantic and malignant female, the Hecate of this mythology, who rode on the storm and marshalled the rambling host of wanderers under her grim banner. This hag (in all respects the reverse of the Mab or Titania of the Celtic creed) was called Nicneven in that later system which blended the faith of the Celts and of the Goths on this subject. The great Scottish poet Dunbar has made a spirited description of this Hecate riding at the head of witches and good neighbours (fairies, namely), sorceresses and elves, indifferently, upon the ghostly eve of All-Hallow Mass. In

Italy, we hear of the hags arraying themselves under the orders of Diana (in her triple character of Hecate, doubtless) and Herodias, who were the joint leaders of their choir, But we return to the more simple fairy belief, as entertained by the Celts before they were conquered by the Saxons."

In John Koch's *Celtic Culture*, we are told:

"The Queen of the Fairies in Scotland, sometimes known as the queen of the witches, was Neven or NicNeven, a name Henderson and Cowan derive from Neamhain, OIr Nemain, a war goddess ... variations on this name are found all over Scotland ..."

Based of the character of the goddess and the implied meanings of her name when used as a common noun, the most likely derivation is as follows:

OIr neim 'poison' (Goth *niman* 'take', etc). n-stem, Mod. Ir. neimh 'poison'. Proto-Celtic *nemen from older *nemn, from PIE root *nem 'to allot'.

From the *Electronic Dictionary of the Irish Language*:

"nemain
Nemain Emain anemain ineamhain némainn
Keywords: war-goddess; battle-fury; warlike; frenzy; strife; murder; malice."

However, both noted Celtic linguist Professor Ranko Matosovic and Dr. Simon Rodway of the University of Wales prefer deriving Nemhain's name from OIr nem, gen nime 'heaven' (Lat nemus, nemoris), Old Irish nem 'holy, heaven' is cognate with Gaul. nemeton, Lat nemus, etc. (from PCelt. *nemo-).

If Nemhain's name can be related to both Diana Nemorensis and the Celtic Nemeton, then Nemhain and Gwenddydd would both be lunar Goddesses. Gwenddydd and the Lady of the Lake would be one and the same deity.

THE WILD MAN OF THE WOOD IN HIGHLAND SCOTLAND

The *Buile Shuibhne* or *'Frenzy of Suibhne'*, which tells the story of the quintessential Irish madman, contains within it an episode that many have thought may be a reference to the British Myrddin (or Merlin). This British madman is called Fer Caille, the 'Man of the Wood' (cf. Geoffrey of Monmouth's 'sylvester homo' for Merlin), or Alladhan (only once Ealadhan). Scholars have debated whether Alladhan is an attempt to render Llallogan, the real name of Myrddin. Some think this might be the case, while others opt for interpreting Alladhan as being derived from Gaelic *allaid(h)*, 'wild', making for 'the Wild One'. The point is rather moot, as I've already demonstrated that the word at the root of Llallogan and *allaid(h)* is, in fact, the same word. Llallogan (Llallog with a diminutive suffix) as 'the Other' and Alladhan as 'the Wild One' are, therefore, much more closely related etymologically than one might otherwise think.

The relevant section of the translated text of *Buile Shuibhne* is here below, taken from ucc.ie/celt/published/T302018/index.html:

"Suibhne then left Carraig Alastair and went over the wide-mouthed, storm-swept sea until he reached the land of the Britons. He left the fortress of the king of the Britons on his right hand and came on a great wood. As he passed along the wood, he heard lamenting and wailing, a great moan of anguish and feeble sighing. It was another madman who was wandering through the wood. Suibhne went up to him. 'Who are you, my man?' said Suibhne. 'I am a madman,' said he. 'If you are a madman,' said Suibhne, 'come hither so that we may be friends, for I too am a madman.' 'I would,' said the other, 'were it not for fear of the king's house or household seizing me, and I do not know that you are not one of them.' 'I am not indeed,' said Suibhne, 'and since I am not, tell me your family name.' 'Fer Caille (Man of the Wood) is my name,' said the madman; whereupon Suibhne uttered this stave and Fer Caille answered him as follows:

Suibhne:
'O Fer Caille, what has befallen thee?
sad is thy voice;
tell me what has marred thee
in sense or form.'

Fer Caille:
'I would tell thee my story,
likewise my deeds,
were it not for fear of the proud host
of the king's household.

Ealadhan am I
who used to go to many combats,
I am known to all
as the leading madman of the glens
[variant: swift madman ...].'

Suibhne:
'Suibhne son of Colman am I,
from the pleasant Bush;
the easier for us is converse
here, O man.'

After that, each confided in the other and they asked tidings of each other. Said Suibhne to the madman: 'Give an account of yourself.' 'I am son of a landholder,' said the madman of Britain, 'and I am a native of this country in which we are, and Alladhan is my name.' 'Tell me,' said Suibhne, 'what caused your madness?' 'Not difficult to say. Once upon a time, two kings were contending for the sovereignty of this country, viz., Eochaidh Aincheas son of Guaire Mathra, and Cugua son of Guaire. Of the people of Eochaidh am I,' said he, 'for he was the better of the two. There was then convened a great assembly to give battle to each other concerning the country. I put geasa on each one of my lord's people that none of them should come to the battle except they were clothed in silk, so that they might be conspicuous beyond all for pomp and pride. The hosts gave three shouts of malediction on me, which sent me wandering and fleeing as you see.'

In the same way, he asked Suibhne what drove him to madness. 'The words of Ronan,' said Suibhne, 'for he cursed me in front of the Battle of Magh Rath, so that I rose on high out of the battle, and I have been wandering and fleeing ever since.' 'O Suibhne,' said Alladhan, 'let each of us keep good watch over the other since we have placed trust in each other; that is, he who shall soonest hear the cry of a heron from a blue-watered, green-watered lough or the clear note of a cormorant, or the flight of a woodcock from a branch, the whistle or sound of a plover on being woke from its sleep, or the sound of withered branches being broken, or shall see the shadow of a bird above the wood, let him who shall first hear warn and tell the other; let there be the distance of two trees between us; and if one of us should hear any of the before-mentioned things or anything resembling them, let us fly quickly away thereafter.'

They do so, and they were a whole year together. At the end of the year, Alladhan said to Suibhne: 'It is time that we part to-day, for the end of my life has come, and I must go to the place where it has been destined for me to die.' 'What death shall you die?' asked Suibhne. 'Not difficult to say,' said Ealladhan; 'I go now to Eas Dubhthaigh, and a blast of wind will get under me and cast me into the waterfall so that I shall be drowned, and I shall be buried afterwards in a churchyard of a saint, and I shall obtain

Heaven; and that is the end of my life. And, O Suibhne,' said Alladhan, 'tell me what your own fate will be.' Suibhne then told him as the story relates below. At that they parted and the Briton set out for Eas Dubhthaigh, and when he reached the waterfall he was drowned in it."

The first thing to be said about this account of Alladhan is that he belongs to the region of the ancient Caledonian Wood in Highland Scotland, NOT to the 'Celyddon Wood' the Welsh placed in Lowland Scotland. We know this because the fort of the king of the Britons Suibhne left on his right hand is Dumbarton, the Dark Age Alclud or Dun Breatann. Of the chieftains involved in the battle that sends Alladhan fleeing, we can say nothing other than that the names are thoroughly Gaelic, not British and not Pictish. Eochaidh is a common Irish name; there were several such in Scottish Dalriada. Aincheas is Irish *aincheas*, found once as a personal name. It meant 'pain, difficulty, trouble, doubt, perplexity', etc. Cugua looks like a truncated form of Cucuach, found in the Annals of Ulster for the year 1166. A Cucuagh spelling may well have lost its terminal. Mathra is Irish *mathra*, *maithre*, 'mother's kin or tribe, maternal kins-folk'. Guaire is another common Irish name.

While the date of *Buile Shuibhne* is roughly placed in the thirteenth-fifteenth centuries, references to it have been found in the tenth century. I now know, having discovered the place of Alladhan's death, that the story cannot have been composed prior to the life of the Scottish saint, Dubthach or Duthac (c.1000–1065).

The waterfall (eas) of Dubhthaigh and the associated saint's churchyard point solidly to the magnificent Falls of Glomach in Kintail, not far to the northeast of Kilduich or Clachan Duich, the church and stone-cell of St. Duthac. Depending on which site one accesses, the Glomach Falls are either the second or third highest in all of Britain. More importantly, the falls can be reached by following a path, part of which follows alongside the River Elchaig, one of the 'coffin roads' used to take the dead to Clachan Duich for Christian burial.

Alladhan would not appear, then, to have anything to do with the Welsh Myrddin/Llallogan – other than the fact that both were spectres or 'madmen'. Christians found it necessary to supply both with deaths and proper burials, either through a misunderstanding of the real meaning of 'madness' in these contexts or as a method of eliminating Pagan aspects from the motif.

SOME OTHER MYSTERIOUS PLACES ASSOCIATED WITH MERLIN

There are some other Merlin sites whose locations are uncertain. Five of them are the Fountain of Barenton, another tomb of Merlin, the spring of Galabes, Merlin's esplumoir and the green chapel of the Gawain poem.

The Fountain of Barenton is none other than the mineral springs of Berrington (Berinton) near Tenbury Wells in Herefordshire.

A previously unlocated grave of Merlin is said by the *Prose Lancelot* to be in the Perilous Forest of Darnantes atop a mountain. Darnantes or Dar-nantes is the River Dore, which flows through the Golden Valley in the Black Mountains of Wales. Dore is either from French D'ore, 'golden', or W. *dwr*, 'water', while –nantes is from W. *nant*, 'stream, brook'. The Perilous Forest of the Dore River must be in this area, which is still forested to this day. Only a couple of miles west of the Dore is Mynydd Merddin, 'Myrddin's Mountain', one of the traditional Welsh sites of Merlin's tomb. However, as Mynydd Merddin is an outlier of the Black Mountains, this could well be a relocation of Merlin's mountain at the Eildons in the north.

As for Merlin's spring or springs of Galabes, Geoffrey of Monmouth places this site in the region of the Gewisse. In a note to his *The Quest for Merlin* (pp.270–1), Tolstoy suggests that Geoffrey may have substituted the Gewisse for Nennius' Guunessi. This would mean, of course, that Galabes would be found in Guunessi. Tolstoy is mistaken here. Merlin's Galabes is plainly Nennius' Guoloph, i.e. Wallop, the site of a battle between Aurelius Ambrosius and Vitalinus. Now there is a Wallop stream in the Shropshire of Vortigern, but there is another in Hampshire, the Wallop Brook, site of the villages known as the Wallops. Hampshire is within the territory of the Gewissei.

The Cair Guorthirgin of Guunessi has been identified with a site at Nant Gwrtheyrn near the northwest coast of Llyn between Yr Eifl and Nefyn. Guunessi (Gwnnws, Gwynnys) is now a farm two miles south of Nant Gwrtheyrn.

Now to treat briefly of the famous 'esplumoir' or 'esplumeor' of Merlin, which the *Didot Perceval* places next to the Grail Castle of Bron and Perceval:

> "... and I wish to make a lodging outside your palace and to dwell there ... And all those who will see my lodging will name it the esplumoir of Merlin ['si le clameront l'esplumoir Merlin']. Then Merlin left them and made his esplumoir and entered within and never since then has he been seen in the world."

Raoul de Houdenc's *Meraugis de Portlesguez* identifies the esplumoir as a high rock upon which are twelve damsels forever prophesying. These 'twelve damsels' are in reality a stone circle. They are akin to various stone circles named for maidens or witches, e.g. Boleigh's Merry Maidens, Bosscawen-Un's Nine Maidens, Little Selkeld's Long Meg and Her Daughters, Harthill Moor's Grey Ladies, Stanton's Nine Ladies.

The best guess to date as to the meaning of esplumoir is 'moulting cage', but this is usually considered unsatisfactory. The word is otherwise unknown in Old French.

The es- of esplumoir is a prefix such as that added to caliber to form Escalibur or Excalibur, the name of Arthur's sword in later romance. As such, it can be dropped, leaving us with a word spelled 'plumoir' or 'plumeor'. I would see in either of these an obvious Old French attempt at Old Breton *ploe*, 'parish', plus *meur*, 'great'. There are four Ploemeur place-names in Brittany: Pleumeur-Bodou and Pleumeur-Gautier in Cotes d'Armor, Plomeur in Finistere, and Ploemeur in Morbihan. Plomeur in Finistere is home to the Kerugou dolmen.

Suppose, however, that 'great parish' is not being used in this context as a genuine place-name, but as a description of a type of district. I believe this, is in fact, what the author of the *Didot Perceval* intends here. He was availing himself of two traditions. One, which is known to come from before the twelfth century, is the designation of the island of Britain as 'Clas Merdin'. Clas, according to the Geiriadur Prifysgol Cymru, has the meanings: 'monastic community, monastica classis, cloister, people of the same country, band or community of fellow-countrymen'. The second strand of tradition comes from Geoffrey of Monmouth, who makes Amesbury the scene of a famous monastery, the so-called Cloister of Ambrius (or Emrys, the Welsh form of the Latin name Ambrosius). This monastery may be referred to in the *Welsh Triads* under its name Caer Caradoc, one of the three eternal choirs of the island of Britain. This again is due to Geoffrey, who refers to Salisbury near Stonehenge and Amesbury as Caer Caradoc.

Geoffrey, furthermore, places Stonehenge or the Giants' Dance atop a hill next to the parish of Amesbury, supposedly the 'Fort of Ambrosius'. For Geoffrey, and anyone reading him in the Middle Ages, Ambrosius was merely another name for Merlin himself.

The 'Great Parish' of Merlin, i.e. of Ambrosius, would be the parish of Amesbury with its stone circle. Again, according to Geoffrey, Ambrosius brother of Uther was buried within the Giant's Dance. Since Merlin bears the Ambrosius name as well, the *Didot Perceval* author placed Merlin's Otherworld 'lodging' or tomb at Stonehenge.

But if the Esplumeor Merlin = the 'great parish' of Amesbury, then the nearby Grail Castle obviously was not Corbenic or Castell Dinas Bran in North Wales, a tradition recorded in other Arthurian romances (see https://secretsavalon.blogspot.com/2016/08/the-holy-grail-of-arthurian-tradition.html).

Then what is the Grail Castle next to the Great Parish of Ambrosius?

The best guess would be Amesbury's neighbouring hillfort, Vespasian's Camp, only 1.2 miles east of Stonehenge.

The name of this camp is due to the Elizabethan antiquarian Camden. In reality, the fort pre-dates the Romans. However, I think it is not a coincidence that Geoffrey of Monmouth calls Salisbury Caer Caradoc after the British chieftain Caractacus who was defeated by the Roman Vespasian. We have no record of Salisbury ever being referred to as the fort of Caractacus; the ancient name of Old Sarum next to Salisbury was Sorviodunum.

Could not Geoffrey have mistaken Salisbury the town for Caer Caradoc, when in reality Caer Caradoc was the name of the hillfort on Salisbury Plain? Camden might well have replaced the name of the defeated British chieftain with that of the Roman conqueror, Vespasian. If so, the 'eternal choir' of Caer Caradoc mentioned in the *Welsh Triads* is another name for the Cloister of Ambrosius at Amesbury. And as far as the author of the *Didot Perceval* was concerned, Vespasian's Camp next to the Esplumeor Merlin or Great Parish of Amesbury was the Grail Castle.

Another Arthurian site has always intrigued me; that of the green chapel in the fourteenth-century epic poem, *Sir Gawain and the Green Knight*. While it is not immediately apparent that the green chapel has anything to do with Merlin, we will see that it actually belongs to the great enchanter.

The poem leaves no doubt as to what the green chapel really is:

> "... a hillock of sorts, A smooth-surfaced barrow on a slope beside a stream ... All hollow it was within, only an old cavern ..." (Lines 2171-82).

This chambered barrow is 'hardly two miles' from the castle of the Green Knight, who calls himself Bertilak of Hautdesert (High Desert). The directions to this castle are unknown; we are only told that Gawain is going north by way of the Gwynedd coast opposite Anglesey and the Wirral Peninsula. After this, the description of his route becomes increasingly vague.

Bertilak represents the Bertholais of the Arthurian Vulgate. Indeed, the English translation of the Vulgate renders Bertholais as Bertilak. This Bertholais is associated with Gawain, but does not bear any of the characteristics later ascribed to Bertilak. In the Vulgate, Bertholais and the False Guinevere (whose champion the former was) are exiled to the hinterlands. The suggestion has been made that Bertilak's beautiful wife, the temptress of Gawain, is actually the False Guinevere. Because the poet put Morgan le Fay in Bertilak's house, it is also possible that the Green Knight's wife is an aspect of Morgen, i.e. the Morrigan.

Bertholais owes his name to the Britaelis of Geoffrey of Monmouths *History*. Britaelis was Gorlois' servant whose form was assumed by none other than Merlin in the story of Ygerna's seduction by Uther. If Bertholais is Merlin, it is surely significant that *The Life of St. Kentigern* has Lailoken/Myrddin/Merlin buried 'not far from the [barrow] mound where the brook Pausayl flows into the River Tweed.' In other words, the 'green chapel' is none other than the site of the Scottish Lowland Merlin's supposed grave at Highmoat.

In the Vulgate Merlin, the forest name of the Lady of the Lake is first given as the Forest of Briosque and only later as Broceliande, the name used by Chretien de Troyes. While Broceliande has been sought in various places, none of the candidates work geographically or etymologically. I would derive the Old French 'Briosque' from the –fries component of Dumfries, the town situated just west-southwest of Lochmaben in Dumfriesshire. While once thought to be the 'Fort of the Frisians', authorities now correctly identify –fries with Gaelic *preas*, Angl. Pres(s), gen. phris, Angl. –fries, gen. pl. preas, (b)p(h)reasach, 'bush, copse, thicket'. Spellings such as Dunfreisch, Droonfreisch, and Drumfriesche occasionally occur in old documents.

The second component is probably something similar to Welsh *llwyn*:

[bnth. Llad. lignum, cf. H. Lyd. loin, loen mewn e. lleoedd, ?Crn. Diw. loinou (ll.)]

eg. (bach. g. llwynyn, ll. llwynynnau) ll. llwynau, llwyni, llwynydd (bach. ll. (prin) llwynïos), 'bush, shrub, brake, thicket; copse, grove, arbour; woods, forest; (esp. in love-poetry) the traditional rendezvous of lovers, symbol of love or romance'.

Broceliande itself may be evident in compounds like Welsh *prysglwyn*, 'shrub, shrubbery, bush, brake, undergrowth, thicket, copse, jungle, also fig' and *brysglwyn*, 'thicket, copse, brushwood'.

It makes a great deal of sense to envisage Merlin and Viviane in the Dumfries region, as this was the home stomping grounds of Myrddin, the Welsh prototype for Geoffrey of Monmouth's Merlin. Nefyn/Nemhain = Viviane, and the Welsh made Nefyn the mother of Urien of Rheged, the center of which was Annandale (see https://mistshadows.blogspot.com/2017/09/

the-nucleus-of-uriens-kingdom-of-rheged.html). Broceliande, then, is simply a name for Dumfries.

In the context of any discussion of Myrddin and Nemhain in southwest Scotland, it is necessary to mention the Locus Maponi or 'place of [the god] Maponus', identifiable with Lochmaben in Dumfries (or perhaps the Ladyward Roman fort near Lochmaben, or even with the Clochmabenstane just south at Gretna Green). As is well known, Mabon was the son of Modron, i.e. Matrona, the Divine Mother. This is the same Modron who is presented as the wife of Urien, son of Nyfain/Nemhain.

There is a strong probability that the 'stone' under which Merlin was imprisoned by the Lady of the Lake in Broceliande is none other than the Clochmabenstane [I would note, however, that there is a lost chapel of Munmaban where we now find the Harestanes stone circle near Kirkurd in Peebleshire].

MYRDDIN AND THE JOURNEY TO AVALON

The very first account of Arthur's conveyance to Avalon differs remarkably from that found in late sources such as the *Morte D'Arthur* of Sir Thomas Malory. It is Geoffrey of Monmouth's *Life of Merlin* that tells us how Arthur was brought by boat from Camlann to Avalon, with Merlin a passenger and Barinthus the steersman. As has been recognized for some time, this Barinthus is Geoffrey's spelling for the famous Irish St. Brendan the Navigator, originally Breanainn, who set out from Ireland to find Tir Tairngire or the Land of Promise in the west.

The typical Celtic triad of Arthur, Merlin/Myrddin and Barinthus/Brendan is replaced in the romances by various numbers of 'queens', i.e. goddesses of Avalon, who ferry Arthur away to the Otherworld without any masculine assistance. Morgan (a Welsh substitute for the Irish Morrigan; see https://secretsavalon.blogspot.com/2016/07/the-mysteries-of-avalon-chapter-two.html) is often listed as one of these 'queens', as is the Lady of the Lake, of course. We've seen that the Lady of the Lake was Nemhain/Gwenddydd/Diana, and we know from the Irish sources that the Morrigan and Nemhain were often paired as battle or sovereignty goddesses. In the Roman period, a Dea Latis or 'Lake Goddess' was worshiped at Avalon, i.e. the Burgh-by-Sands Roman fort (Aballava/Avalana/'Avalon').

Breanainn is a borrowing from the Welsh and is a name based on *brenin*, 'king'. Brenin itself derives from the name of the goddess Brigantia, specifically from *brigantinos, a term which identified the king or 'exalted one' as consort of the tutelary goddess of the Brigantes tribe. As the Camlann that was Castlesteads and the Avalon that was Burgh-by-Sands are both in Carvetii territory, and the Carvetii were part of the Brigantian confederation, it is particularly appropriate that the pilot of the boat should bear this name.

Of course, we are talking about ancient religious symbolism here – not physical fact. It is well known that Myrddin (if a man and not a god) lived and died well after Arthur's time. He could not, therefore, have been personally present in the funeral barge that took Arthur to Avalon. But as Myrddin was a divine spirit of a slain warrior-bard, he may be emblematic of the other slain champions who perished with Arthur at Camlann and who, presumably, also were taken to Avalon – either literally or metaphorically.

MYRDDIN AND THE GODS MABON AND LLEU

Up until this point, I have resisted seeing Myrddin as a sort of dethroned Pagan god, perhaps Maponus, the Welsh Mabon, and/or Lleu. And I will continue to do so, as I prefer to see him as a Lleu avatar. However, there is no doubt that elements derived from relics of Celtic religion did adhere to him.

The Welsh appear to have identified Mabon/Maponus with Lleu. I've discussed this in detail elsewhere, as well as the misidentification of these conflated gods with Ambrosius. See, for example, https://secretsavalon.blogspot.com/2016/10/a-forgotten-bit-on-emrys-ball-player.html. Yet my resistance to accepting Myrddin as strictly a sun deity stems from the fact that all the 'god qualities' assigned to him originate in Geoffrey of Monmouth's writings and Jocelyn of Furness's hagiographical *Life of St. Kentigern*. Both sources are late and of more than dubious authority.

Geoffrey identifies Myrddin, his 'Merlin', with the Welsh god Lleu – this last having been identified wrongly with Ambrosius, the 'divine or immortal one'. Ambrosius is found a king of Gwynedd in Nennius, while Lleu is the ancient lord of NW Wales in Welsh tradition. *The Life of Kentigern*, either aware of this tradition or drawing from some unknown material, assigns a triple death to Myrddin not unlike that suffered by Lleu in the Welsh *Mabinogion*. Many modern theorists have, therefore, tended to identify Myrddin with Lleu. We should recall that the people of Drumelzier near Louden Knowe – the Hill of Lugh's Fort – were the 'Reapers', and so we might wonder if the killing of Myrddin (if Lugh or a Lugh surrogate or avatar) coincided with the reaping of the first grain on Lughnasadh.

The triple sacrifice of Lleu would have been enacted every year. Lleu's annual death occurred originally at February 1st or Imbolc, if calculated around 1200 AD, the approximate date of the composition of the MABINOGION. The goat and bathtub of Lleu's death scene represent, respectively, the goat of Capricorn and the water-bearer of Aquarius. In 3000 BCE, the sun was between these two signs on the winter solstice.

Taking all of the above into account, I must conclude that while it cannot be proven Myrddin was originally the sun god Maponus/Lleu, it is certainly possible that a deity has been superimposed upon a figure who started out, at any rate, as the mortal man Myrddin/Llallogan.

Alternately, we could view Myrddin as an AVATAR of the god Lleu. The avatar concept – that of a deity who assumes human form – is a difficult one for us in the West to grapple with. In simple terms, Myrddin came to be seen as a sacred warrior, one dedicated to Lleu. When he died in battle or was sacrificed prior to it, he became 'one' with the god. Sacrifice victims symbolized the god to whom they were given. For example, men sacrificed to Odin by hanging represented the god himself as he hung from the World Tree. As a Lleu warrior or chieftain, Myrddin could be viewed as the sun god incarnate.

The only other circle which could conceivably have been associated with Myrddin is the one that, apparently, once existed at the Clochmabenstone.

https://canmore.org.uk/site/67441/lochmaben-stone

The description of the non-extant circle here does not, however, match that given for Gwenddydd's house in Monmouth's *Vita Merlini*. Still, given the Mabon-Lleu conflation in Welsh tradition, and the proximity of Clochmabenstone to Arthuret, it has to remain a candidate. Certainly, Geoffrey was not beyond exaggerating for the sake of his tale, and I've already suggested above that a stone circle in Cumbria or Dumfriesshire could have been linked to Stonehenge.

We should also bear in mind in this context (see above) that the stone of Broceliande, under which Merlin is imprisoned by the Lady of the Lake, may well be the Clochmabenstone. Or it could be some other notable chambered tomb in Dumfriesshire – of which there are plenty to choose from.

Aurelius Ambrosius, said to be a Roman, is the most famous figure in Dark Age British history prior to Arthur. Why? Because he is credited with having united the Britons in a successful defense of the country against the Saxons, who from Vortigern's time had, according to the traditional account, pillaged and conquered at will.

Ambrosius is important also because it has been fashionable to identify him with Arthur. As we shall see, such an identification is patently impossible.

To begin, Ambrosius was not a contemporary of Arthur. He was not, in fact, even a contemporary of Vortigern, who preceded Arthur by a century. And this is true despite the *HB* account, which brings Vortigern and Ambrosius (as the Welsh Emrys) together for a fabulous story that takes place at Dinas Emrys in northwestern Wales (see below).

There are major problems with accepting Ambrosius as a contemporary of Vortigern. First, he cannot have been a Roman and been in Britain during or after Vortigern's rule. The withdrawal of the Romans is firmly dated at c.409 CE. Vortigern's ruling dates, depending on the sources consulted, are anywhere from 20 to 40 years after the Roman withdrawal. If he were a Roman during or after Vortigern, then he came from the Continent and was not a native Briton. The argument could be made that 'Romanized' Britons continued to preserve the Roman way of life in southern England for a half-century after the withdrawal of the troops. In this sense, a chieftain like Ambrosius might still consider himself to be 'Roman'.

However, the *HB* tells us that Ambrosius fought a battle against a certain Vitalinus at a Guoloph or Wallop, thought to be the Hampshire Wallop. This Vitalinus is listed in the *HB* as the grandfather of Vortigern. This means that Ambrosius has wrongly been placed in the time of Vortigern. He actually belongs to the time of Vitalinus, who was probably of the fourth century.

The father of the famous fourth-century St. Ambrose bore the name Aurelius Ambrosius. This man was, furthermore, the prefect or governor of Gaul (Gallia). Britain, Spain and Gaul were in the Gallic prefecture. So, we have here a historical figure named Aurelius Ambrosius who not only was a true 'Roman', but who could have had something to do with military operations carried out in Britain in the fourth century.

There is good reason to believe that St. Ambrose himself bore the name Aurelius. Jones' *Prosopography of the Later Roman Empire* gives no second name for the Bishop of Milan, and neither does Paulinus of Milan's *Vita*. Ambrose may have belonged to the gens Aurelia, as we know that he was related to Symmachus [Quintus Aurelius Symmachus]; an inscription refers to him as Au-relius Ambrosius. It is true that there is a debate over the Ambrose referred to in the inscription. Those who think it is Ambrose junior [St. Am-brose] point out that a dedication to St. Nazarius is involved. The point may be moot: if Ambrose senior belonged to the gens Aurelia, so did the son, and vice versa. Incidentally, St. Ambrose's Milan was anciently called Mediolanum, and there was also a Roman town of this name in the British Cornovii tribal territory.

One other factor strongly indicates that there is no good historical reason for accepting a fifth-century Aurelius Ambrosius in Britain. Vortigern's only interaction with Ambrosius, or Emrys Guletic ('Prince Ambrosius'), as he is called in Welsh tradition, is in the Dinas Emrys folktale already alluded to above.

Other than Dinas Emrys, there appears to be no site in Britain which can be shown to contain the personal name Ambrosius. Still, this hero may even have been placed at Guoloph/Wallop because of the proximity of this stream to Amesbury. As Geoffrey of Monmouth did much later, Ambrosius's name was fancifully associated with Amesbury.

The town name does not, in fact, seem to contain the personal name Ambrosius. Its etymology is, instead, as follows:

> Ambresbyrig, from a c.880 CE charter, then various spellings to Amblesberie in Domesday. Almost certainly a personal name, Ambre or Aembre, cognate with the Old German Ambri, hence Ambre's burgh, cf. Ombersley. All the early

forms for Amesbury have the medial -b-, but no form has any extension that would justify derivation from Ambrosius.

Ambrosius as a Latin adjective means 'the Divine or Immortal One'. As such, it was at some point taken to be a title for the Welsh god Lleu. Welsh tradition made Lleu the ancient ruler of Gwynedd, and this is the rank granted to Emrys or Ambrosius in the HB. Hence, Dinas Emrys in northwestern Wales, the '[Hill-] fort of the Divine or Immortal One', is actually the fort of Lleu.

The Welsh also appear to have identified the youthful god Mabon with Lleu. That this is so is demonstrated by the placement of the two gods in death at the same place. According to the *Mabinogion* tale, *Math Son of Mathonwy*, Lleu is found as the death-eagle in the oak tree at Nantlle (Nant Lleu) in Snowdonia, not far from Dinas Emrys. And one of the Stanzas of the Graves reads:

> "The grave on Nantlle's height, No one knows its attributes – Mabon son of Modron the Swift."

Geoffrey of Monmouth proceeded to further confuse the story of Ambrosius, a Roman governor of Gaul mistakenly identified with a Welsh god, by identifying both with the northern Myrddin or Merlin. Hence, we find Merlin or 'Merlin Ambrosius' in the Dinas Emrys story of Emrys/Lleu/Mabon.

In addition, Merlin is placed at the springs of Galabes, Geoffrey's attempt at the Guoloph of the hero Ambrosius.

In conclusion, we can only say that there is no good reason for supposing that Vortigern and Ambrosius were contemporaries. Instead, the Ambrosius mentioned by Gildas as having military success in Britian must have been the fourth-century Gallic governor of that name. This being the case, Ambrosius could not possibly have been the victor at the Battle of Mount Badon, which is dated 516 CE. And, by extension, Ambrosius was not Arthur.

THE GHOST AMBROSIUS OR WHY ARTHUR'S PREDECESSOR SHOULD BE STRICKEN FROM THE ANNALS OF BRITISH HISTORY

Over the past several years, I've written a handful of articles on Ambrosius Aurelianus, a geographically and temporally dislocated figure in early British legend. Yet despite the evidence I've presented, Arthurian scholars, professional and amateur alike, continue to mistake him for a real personage of fifth-century Britain. The idea that he might even be Arthur is still out there. I feel, therefore, that it is time for a summary treatment of this supposed military hero. The easiest way for me to do this is to itemize the points of my argument:

1) The name of A.A. matches perfectly that of the fourth-century governor of Gaul (whose territo-ries included those of Britain) and his famous son, St. Ambrose. Vortigern's grandfather Vitalinus is said to have fought A.A. at Wallop in Hampshire. Such a battle reference puts A.A. well before Vortigern and negates the possibility that A.A. was a boy during Vortigern's reign.
2) The Campus Elleti of Ambrosius in Wales, where Vortigern's men are said to have found the boy, is also found as Palud or 'marsh' of Elleti in the *Book of Llandaf*. The place is a relocation for the continental Arelate (from *Are-*, 'in front of' + *late*, 'marsh'), the late capital of the Gallic prefecture, which included Britain.
3) Dinas Emrys is a relocation for Amesbury, the latter thought (wrongly) to contain the name of Ambrosius. Dinas Emrys was placed in Eryri because this mountain range was fancifully connected to the Welsh word for eagle, and both St. Ambrose and Magnus the Tyrant (easily confused with Vortigern) are known to have been at Aquileia, a place-name that could have been incorrectly linked with the Latin word for eagle.

4) Trier was in Gallia Belgica, 'Gaul of the Belgae', and A.A.'s Wallop in Hampshire was in the ancient tribal territory of the British Belgae. Gallia could be used in medieval sources for both Gaul and Wales.
5) A.A. is said to have been given Dinas Emrys and the western kingdoms of Britain by Vortigern. This is impossible, as Gwynedd belonged to Cunedda and his sons. This is obviously a mistake for Amesbury, which was inside of what was to become Wessex, the kingdom of the WEST Saxons.
6) A.A. appears to have been identified in folk belief with the god Lleu, styled Lord of Gwyn-edd, who was himself identified by the Welsh with the god Mabon. The Campus Elleti ball-game story is perfectly paralleled in the Irish story of *Mac Og*, the '*Young Son*', the Gaelic version of Mabon.
7) A.A. was further identified with Merlin (Myrddin); himself possibly a form of Lleu or an avatar of that god.

In conclusion, the Ambrosius Aurelianus who first appears in the pages of Gildas is a purely legendary figure, based on the known historical Ambrosii of the continent. He was mistakenly transferred to Britain during the normal course of folklore development, largely due to a confusion of place-names. There is no reason to believe that either Ambrosius – father or son – ever set foot on British soil. To concoct some famous war-leader of the Britons who happened to have been named after one of the Ambrosii is to ignore points 1–7 above.

www.ingramcontent.com/pod-product-compliance
Lightning Source LLC
Chambersburg PA
CBHW061305110426
42742CB00012BA/2063